WHAT HAPPENS IN CORINTH

Titles in the Seedbed Daily Text series:

WHAT HAPPENS IN CORINTH

1 Corinthians

J. D. WALT

Printed in the United States of America

Cover and page design by Strange Last Name
Page layout by PerfecType, Nashville, Tennessee

Walt, J. D. (John David)
  What happens in Corinth : 1 Corinthians / J.D. Walt. – Franklin, Tennessee : Seedbed Publishing, ©2021.

      pages ; cm. – (The Seedbed daily text)

      ISBN 9781628248418 (paperback)
      ISBN 9781628248425 (Mobi)
      ISBN 9781628248432 (ePub)
      ISBN 9781628248449 (uPDF)

      1. Bible. Corinthians, 1st--Meditations. 2. Spiritual exercises.
      I. Title. II. Series.

BS2675.45.W34 2021   242/.2   2021931213

SEEDBED PUBLISHING
Franklin, Tennessee
seedbed.com

Contents

An Invitation to Awakening

This resource comes with an invitation.

The invitation is as simple as it is comprehensive. It is not an invitation to commit your life to this or that cause or to join an organization or to purchase another book. The invitation is this: to wake up to the life you always hoped was possible and the reason you were put on planet Earth.

It begins with following Jesus Christ. In case you are unaware, Jesus was born in the first century BCE into a poor family from Nazareth, a small village located in what is modern-day Israel. While his birth was associated with extraordinary phenomena, we know little about his childhood. At approximately thirty years of age, Jesus began a public mission of preaching, teaching, and healing throughout the region known as Galilee. His mission was characterized by miraculous signs and wonders; extravagant care of the poor and marginalized; and multiple unconventional claims about his own identity and purpose. In short, he claimed to be the incarnate Son of God with the mission and power to save people from sin, deliver them from death, and bring them into the now and eternal kingdom of God—on earth as it is in heaven.

In the spring of his thirty-third year, during the Jewish Passover celebration, Jesus was arrested by the religious authorities, put on trial in the middle of the night, and at their urging, sentenced to death by a Roman governor. On the day known to history as Good Friday, Jesus was crucified on a Roman cross. He was buried in a borrowed tomb. On the following Sunday, according to multiple eyewitness accounts, he was physically raised from the dead. He appeared to hundreds of people, taught his disciples, and prepared for what was to come.

Forty days after the resurrection, Jesus ascended bodily into the heavens where, according to the Bible, he sits at the right hand of God, as the Lord of heaven and earth. Ten days after his ascension, in a gathering of more than three thousand people on the Day of Pentecost, a Jewish day of celebration, something truly extraordinary happened. A loud and powerful wind swept over the people gathered. Pillars of what appeared to be fire descended upon the followers of Jesus. The Holy Spirit, the presence and power of God, filled the people, and the church was born. After this, the followers of Jesus went forth and began to do the very things Jesus did—preaching, teaching, and healing—planting churches and making disciples all over the world. Today, more than two thousand years later, the movement has reached us. This is the Great Awakening, and it has never stopped.

Yes, two thousand years hence and more than two billion followers of Jesus later, this awakening movement of Jesus Christ and his church stands stronger than ever. Billions of ordinary people the world over have discovered in Jesus Christ an awakened life they never imagined possible. They have overcome challenges, defeated addictions, endured untenable hardships and suffering with unexplainable joy, and stared death in the face with the joyful confidence of eternal life. They have healed the sick, gathered the outcasts, embraced the oppressed, loved the poor, contended for justice, labored for peace, cared for the dying, and, yes, even raised the dead.

We all face many challenges and problems. They are deeply personal, yet when joined together, they create enormous and complex chaos in the world, from our hearts to our homes to our churches and our cities. All of this chaos traces to two originating problems: sin and death. Sin, far beyond mere moral failure, describes the fundamental broken condition of every human being. Sin separates us from God and others, distorts and destroys our deepest identity as the image-bearers of God, and poses a fatal problem from which we cannot save ourselves. It results in an ever-diminishing quality of life and ultimately ends in eternal death. Because Jesus lived a life of sinless perfection, he is able to save us from sin and restore us to a right relationship with God, others, and ourselves. He did this through his sacrificial death on the cross on our behalf. Because Jesus rose from the dead, he is able to deliver us from death and bring us into a quality of life both eternal and unending.

This is the gospel of Jesus Christ: pardon from the penalty of sin, freedom from the power of sin, deliverance from the grip of death, and awakening to the supernatural empowerment of the Holy Spirit to live powerfully for the good of others and the glory of God. Jesus asks only that we acknowledge our broken selves as failed sinners, trust him as our Savior, and follow him as our Lord. Following Jesus does not mean an easy life; however, it does lead to a life of power and purpose, joy in the face of suffering, and profound, even world-changing, love for God and people.

All of this is admittedly a lot to take in. Remember, this is an invitation. Will you follow Jesus? Don't let the failings of his followers deter you. Come and see for yourself.

Here's a prayer to get you started:

> Our Father in heaven, it's me (say your name), I want to know you. I want to live an awakened life. I confess I am a sinner. I have failed myself, others, and you in many ways. I know you made me for a purpose and I want to fulfill that purpose with my one life. I want to follow Jesus Christ. Jesus, thank you for the gift of your life and death and resurrection and ascension on my behalf. I want to walk in relationship with you as Savior and Lord. Would you lead me into the fullness and newness of life I was made for? I am ready to follow you. Come, Holy Spirit, and fill me with the love, power, and purposes of God. I pray these things by faith in the name of Jesus, amen.

It would be our privilege to help you get started and grow deeper in this awakened life of following Jesus. For some next steps and encouragements, visit seedbed.com/awaken.

How the Daily Text Works

It seems obvious to say, but the Daily Text is written every day. Mostly it is written the day before it is scheduled to release online.

Before you read further, you are cordially invited to subscribe to and receive the daily e-mail. Visit seedbed.com/dailytext to get started. Also, check out the popular Facebook group, Seedbed Daily Text.

Eventually, the daily postings become part of a Daily Text discipleship resource. That's what you hold in your hands now.

It's not exactly a Bible study, though the Bible is both the source and subject. You will learn something about the Bible along the way: its history, context, original languages, and authors. The goal is not educational in nature, but transformational. Seedbed is more interested in folks knowing Jesus than knowing *about* Jesus.

To that end, each reading begins with the definitive inspiration of the Holy Spirit, the ongoing, unfolding text of Scripture. Following that is a short and, hopefully, substantive insight from the text and some aspect of its meaning. For insight to lead to deeper influence, we turn the text into prayer. Finally, influence must run its course toward impact. This is why we ask each other questions. These questions are not designed to elicit information but to crystallize intention.

Discipleship always leads from inspiration to intention and from attention to action.

Using the Daily Text as a Discipleship Curricular Resource for Groups

While Scripture always addresses us personally, it is not written to us individually. The content of Scripture cries out for a community to address. The Daily Text is made for discipleship in community. This resource can work in several different ways. It could be read like a traditional book, a few pages or chapters at a time. Though unadvisable, the readings could be crammed in on the night before the meeting. Keep in mind, the Daily Text is not called the Daily Text for kicks. We believe Scripture is worthy of our most focused and consistent attention. Every day. We all have misses, but let's make every day more than a noble aspiration. Let's make it our covenant with one another.

For Use with Bands

In our judgment, the best and highest use of the Daily Text is made through what we call banded discipleship. A band is a same-gender group of three to five people who read together, pray together, and meet together to become the love of God for one another and the world. With banded discipleship, the daily readings serve more as a common text for the band and grist for the interpersonal conversation mill between meetings. The band meeting is reserved for the specialized activities of high-bar discipleship.

To learn more about bands and banded discipleship, visit discipleshipbands.com. Be sure to download the free *Discipleship Bands: A Practical Field Guide* or order a supply of the printed booklets online. Also be sure to explore Discipleship Bands, our native app designed specifically for the practice of banded discipleship, in the App Store or Google Play.

For Use with Classes and Small Groups

The Daily Text has also proven to be a helpful discipleship resource for a variety of small groups, from community groups to Sunday school classes. Here are some suggested guidelines for deploying the Daily Text as a resource for a small group or class setting:

1. Hearing the Text

Invite the group to settle into silence for a period of no less than one and no more than five minutes. Ask an appointed person to keep time and to read the biblical text covering the period of days since the last group meeting. Allow at least one minute of silence following the reading of the text.

2. Responding to the Text

Invite anyone from the group to respond to the reading by answering these prompts: What did you hear? What did you see? What did you otherwise sense from the Lord?

3. Sharing Insights and Implications for Discipleship

Moving in an orderly rotation (or free-for-all), invite people to share insights and implications from the week's readings.

What did you find challenging, encouraging, provocative, comforting, invasive, inspiring, corrective, affirming, guiding, or warning? Allow group conversation to proceed at will. Limit to one sharing item per turn, with multiple rounds of discussion.

4. Shaping Intentions for Prayer

Invite each person in the group to share a single discipleship intention for the week ahead. It is helpful if the intention can also be framed as a question the group can use to check in from the prior week. At each person's turn, he or she is invited to share how their intention went during the previous week. The class or group can open and close their meeting according to their established patterns.

Introduction

What happens in Corinth . . .

If you live in the United States, the phrase will jump off the page and immediately remind you of the slogan from which it echoes: What happens in Vegas . . .

Of course, the unsaid ending to the phrase is, "stays in Vegas." It's why the unfortunate alias for Las Vegas is Sin City. Sin loves secrecy.

As you will soon learn on the journey into this ancient city and its tiny church, Corinth may well have been the ancient precursor to modern-day Las Vegas (or at least akin to its caricatured reputation).

Here's what most amazes me about this whole project of Paul's first letter to the Corinthians. Paul was writing to a fledgling community of about 150 people in a city of 150,000. And these 150 weren't exactly the cream of the crop. As we will see only a few verses in, this little band of believers were a hot mess. Paul doesn't spend any time wishing for a better church. He works with what God gave him. He knows it only takes a few truly consecrated souls to turn the world upside down. It's why he opens his letter (and we will open every single day) with these words, "To those sanctified in Christ Jesus and called to be his holy people" (i.e., us).

It reminds me of the famous quotation by John Wesley as he looked out on the lost country of England.

> Give me one hundred preachers who fear nothing but sin, and desire nothing but God, and I care not a straw whether they be clergymen or laymen; such alone will shake the gates of hell and set up the kingdom of heaven on Earth.*

Though what happens in Vegas may stay in Vegas, what happened in Corinth has reached the entire world. Sin loves secrecy, but the gospel of Jesus Christ cannot stay quiet. This ancient correspondence to the Corinthian church will lead us on a winding journey of constant interplay between profound truth and practical (and often painful) problems. We will find their problems look a lot like our problems, and along the way we will hear the gospel in ways both delighting and confounding. From the foolishness of the cross to the most sublime teaching on love, some of the most celebrated texts in all of Scripture come out of this letter. Indeed, Paul's Holy Spirit–inspired letter will take us from rigorous perversion to the power of the resurrection within the span of a few chapters. And despite his gift of rhetorical precision, here's where Paul stands through every word:

> And so it was with me, brothers and sisters. When I came to you, I did not come with eloquence or human wisdom as I proclaimed to you the testimony about

---

* John Wesley, writing at age eighty-seven to Alexander Mather, quoted in Luke Tyerman, *The Life and Times of the Rev. John Wesley* (London, 1871), III:632.

God. For I resolved to know nothing while I was with you except Jesus Christ and him crucified. I came to you in weakness with great fear and trembling. My message and my preaching were not with wise and persuasive words, but with a demonstration of the Spirit's power, so that your faith might not rest on human wisdom, but on God's power. (1 Cor. 2:1–5)

Grab a few friends. Pop some popcorn. Get ready for some fireworks. And buckle up. Jesus is coming to Corinth, and to Vegas and to your town, and, yes, what happens after that will go everywhere.

WHAT HAPPENS IN CORINTH

What Happens in Corinth . . .

1 CORINTHIANS 1:1–3 | Paul, called to be an apostle of Christ Jesus by the will of God, and our brother Sosthenes,

To the church of God in Corinth, to those sanctified in Christ Jesus and called to be his holy people, together with all those everywhere who call on the name of our Lord Jesus Christ—their Lord and ours:

Grace and peace to you from God our Father and the Lord Jesus Christ.

Consider This

What happens in Corinth . . . ?

Okay, so a lot happens in Corinth. And, no, it doesn't stay in Corinth. In fact, what happened in Corinth has made it all the way to your city, your home, your e-mail inbox, or your podcast feed. Welcome to this Daily Text series exploring God's Word to the ancient Corinthians, and the present-day Americans, and Kenyans, and Russians, and Brazilians, and Mexicans, and Australians, and Italians, and Ukranians, and Haitians, and you get it.

Words create worlds. Words redeem worlds. And words recreate worlds. In the beginning, God spoke words and created the world. It was the satanic confusion of God's word that led to the fall of humanity. In the fullness of time, God sent his Son, the Word made flesh, to redeem the world.

We think of the apostle Paul as planting churches, making disciples, traveling, and otherwise suffering in jail for the sake of the gospel as his primary ministry. While this is true, the far greater impact of Paul's mission and ministry has to do with the way he put words together into letters to the first-century churches across the land. Almost all of Paul's letters were written to solve problems and restore order in the lives of men and women in these communities who were in the process of being saved by the grace of God in Jesus Christ.

Paul's words worked (and work) in the power of the Holy Spirit to restructure and recreate the worlds in which these people lived by bringing the wisdom of the gospel to bear on their lives and relationships. We begin today with one of these letters: Paul's letter to the church at Corinth. Over the course of the next ten weeks or so, we will become familiar with the ancient city of Corinth, its people, and the way disciples get made in confusing cultures. In some ways, the ancient Corinthian culture will feel much like our own.

To get started I want to point out Paul's foundational assumption in his work. Look for the common word here:

Paul, called to be an apostle of Christ Jesus by the will of God, and our brother Sosthenes,

To the church of God in Corinth, to those sanctified in Christ Jesus and called to be his holy people, together with all those everywhere who call on the name of our Lord Jesus Christ— their Lord and ours:

Called. Paul is called, and the people who make up the church in Corinth are called. This letter (and all of Paul's letters) are written within this overarching framework and mindset. What does it mean for people to be called? It means a really amazing kind of different.

Paul is writing to the church in Corinth as though they had forgotten their core calling. He is not willing to let them phone it in. He is reminding them they are called, to be holy—to be set apart—not some kind of religious organization, but a group of people who are living out their lives in an amazing kind of different fashion. He knows they don't seem to get this at all, but it doesn't change the way he approaches them. He refuses to consider them as anything other than called.

Paul is not willing to create a category for people in the church who are just kind of there hanging out or who show up every now and then and throw a five in the offering plate. That's just not what the church is. As we will soon see, Paul's letter will quickly get to the business of re-calling the called to their calling.

It's about becoming an amazing kind of different; not about being better than anyone else—just waking up to the beautiful life Jesus calls us into, for all its worth, and living it to the absolute fullest.

The Prayer

Our Father in heaven, thank you for the way you winged your Word into the heart of the ancient city of Corinth; for the way you raised up a band of believers there and called them to become holy, to embrace the amazing kind of different life of Jesus Christ in the power of the Holy Spirit. Thank you for the way you are now winging your Word into my city, my church, my home, and my heart. Enlarge my heart, Lord, and stretch my capacity for your presence. Break me from the inside out, so I might somehow contain the uncontainable gift of yourself. In Jesus' name, amen.

The Questions

- How might we develop a richer idea of what "called to be holy" actually means? Rather than all the holier-than-thou images that come to mind, what if we could categorize our calling to follow Jesus in a distinctively winsome fashion?

2 The Core Calling of Every Christian

1 CORINTHIANS 1:4–9 | I always thank my God for you because of his grace given you in Christ Jesus. For in him you have been enriched in every way—with all kinds of speech and with all knowledge—God thus confirming our testimony about Christ among you. Therefore you do not lack any spiritual gift as you eagerly wait for our Lord Jesus Christ to be revealed. He will also keep you firm to the end, so that you will be blameless on the day of our Lord Jesus Christ. God is faithful, who has called you into fellowship with his Son, Jesus Christ our Lord.

Consider This

A few things we need to understand about our context will help shed light on the letter as we begin to move through it.

About Corinth. Corinth was a first-century boomtown. It was a major seaport and a hub of the Mediterranean. In some sense, all roads led to or through Corinth. Corinth was an ancient precursor to sex, drugs, and rock 'n' roll. Transplant Las Vegas in San Diego and you get a feel for first-century Corinth. This bustling colony of Rome had a population of around 100,000–150,000.

About the church in Corinth. Best we can tell, there were no more than about 150 Christians in Corinth. Paul planted the congregation in around AD 50. Nobody had grown up in the church. These were first-generation believers who had mostly come out of pagan religions and cults. Given the size of the church around the world today at approximately 2 billion people, we need to keep in mind the infinitesimally small size of these early churches. It's extraordinary to consider the ultimate impact they had on the world.

About the letters. You will notice later in the letter that Paul references an earlier letter he had written to the church in Corinth. That letter has never been found. The letter we call 1 Corinthians was likely written in about AD 54. It looks like Paul was writing from Ephesus while working with the young church there.

In 1 Corinthians Paul is responding to the Corinthians' response to Paul's earlier (missing) letter. Then there's 2 Corinthians, which also seems to reference another missing letter. In short, it looks like 1 Corinthians is actually Paul's second letter and 2 Corinthians is actually the fourth one. Bottom line: we aren't reading a book here. We are reading one side of a conversation conducted through letters. And as I previously noted, from the side of the conversation we get to study, the little church in Corinth was a mess. In the characterization of New Testament scholar and friend Michael Halcomb, we are looking at a first-century version of *The Jerry Springer Show*.

In today's text, just nine verses in, we quickly come to the end of the nice, salutary portion of the letter. Paul is employing the faithful sandwich technique. You know what I'm talking about? Start with praise, cut to the hard stuff, and end on a good note. In these early verses, Paul is looking for things to be thankful for as relates to these people. He points out their overabundance of knowledge, gifted speech, and spiritual gifts. He reminds them again of the mission of the Holy Spirit in their midst—to make them strong in the Lord and glorious expressions of the holy love of God in the world he sent his Son to save.

Remember their calling? It bears revisiting. "To the church of God in Corinth, to those sanctified in Christ Jesus and called to be his holy people, together with all those everywhere who call on the name of our Lord Jesus Christ—their Lord and ours" (1 Cor. 1:2).

Let's stretch this verse out like a banner over the whole letter. We readily want to interpret our calling as something God wants us to do for him. That is actually the fruit of our calling. Our calling is not to do something; it's to become someone. It is to become someone who, through the power of their life, words, deeds, and relationships, reminds other people of Jesus.

Let's be very clear—this is why Paul is writing the letter.

Paul has one purpose—for the small but growing group of people in Corinth known as the church to fulfill their calling to become sanctified in Christ Jesus and become God's holy people. This, and only this, will win the ballgame. No amount of team reorganization or new methods or better mission statements will ever do it. E. M. Bounds famously said it best, "The Church is looking for better methods. God is looking for better men."

It will take the Word of God in concert with the Spirit of God to transform people of God into the image of God so they can participate in the will of God to redeem the world for God. If I had to reduce the New Testament to one sentence, that would be it.

Now, did you catch the last part of that text above?

together with all those everywhere who call on the name of our Lord Jesus Christ—their Lord and ours . . .

This letter is also to us. We are included in the group of people known as, "all those everywhere who call on the name of our Lord Jesus Christ."

Let's be paying attention.

The Prayer

Father God, thank you for this little band of first-century Christians we know as the church in Corinth. It is amazing to contemplate how you took 150 people in a city of 150,000 and unleashed the gospel of Jesus. I confess, I have focused so much on what you want me to do for you. I want to humble myself and ask, Who do you want me to become? And I want to ask you to help me become it by the power of your Word and Spirit. In Jesus' name, amen.

The Questions

- The Christian faith and church can be parsed into a hundred different possible priorities. What is the priority for you? For your church? What would it mean for you to respond to your calling to become holy? What would it not mean?

3 How Name-Dropping Works

1 CORINTHIANS 1:10–17 | I appeal to you, brothers and sisters, in the name of our Lord Jesus Christ, that all of you agree with one another in what you say and that there be no divisions among you, but that you be perfectly united in mind and thought. My brothers and sisters, some from Chloe's household have informed me that there are quarrels among you. What I mean is this: One of you says, "I follow Paul"; another, "I follow Apollos"; another, "I follow Cephas"; still another, "I follow Christ."

Is Christ divided? Was Paul crucified for you? Were you baptized in the name of Paul? I thank God that I did not baptize any of you except Crispus and Gaius, so no one can say that you were baptized in my name. (Yes, I also baptized the household of Stephanas; beyond that, I don't remember if I baptized anyone else.) For Christ did not send me to baptize, but to preach the gospel—not with wisdom and eloquence, lest the cross of Christ be emptied of its power.

Consider This

To those sanctified in Christ Jesus and called to be his holy people (i.e., us):

(You will remember I have indicated we needed to keep Paul's big picture in mind as we continue through this letter. The opening text comes from the early salutation of the letter. We need to keep these words—their calling and ours—ever before us.)

There are the ways of the world, and there are the ways of God. It is one of the central themes of Scripture. One of the purest crystallizations of this point comes from the prophet Isaiah.

> "For my thoughts are not your thoughts, neither are your ways my ways," declares the LORD.
>
> "As the heavens are higher than the earth, so are my ways higher than your ways and my thoughts than your thoughts." (Isa. 55:8–9)

The ways and systems of the world are inherently divisive. They are built on broken structures and established through power paradigms. Jesus intends his church to witness to and be an example of the higher ways and higher thoughts of God. It's no surprise that the fledgling church in Corinth is steeped in the ways of the world. Why wouldn't they be. They have been thoroughly formed by the ways of the world. It brings to mind a word Paul wrote to the church at Rome, which interestingly enough he seems to have composed while in Corinth. "Do not conform to the pattern of this world, but be transformed by the renewing of your mind. Then you will be able to test and approve what God's will is—his good, pleasing and perfect will" (Rom. 12:2).

I don't want to oversimplify this, yet it is not that complicated. There are the patterns of the world, and there are the patterns of the gospel.

The young Christians at Corinth are doing what immature Christians tend to do. They are importing their ways and means of understanding and doing things into the church. Their culture was steeped in "wisdom" presented by impressive teachers who spoke with great eloquence and with impressive rhetorical style. It was culturally respectable and brought respectability to its adherents. People drafted honor and prestige from these teachers. They claimed importance and distinction by virtue of the importance and distinction of their leaders. It was a constant game of one-upmanship, and it divided people into cliques who likely engaged in all manner of name-dropping and operated in all sorts of under-handed passive-aggressive patterns of behavior.

What I mean is this: One of you says, "I follow Paul"; another, "I follow Apollos"; another, "I follow Cephas"; still another, "I follow Christ."

Paul was not going to let himself get sucked into this. Rather than making this about personalities and critiquing the approaches of other people, Paul cuts to the core issue.

For Christ did not send me to baptize, but to preach the gospel—not with wisdom and eloquence, lest the cross of Christ be emptied of its power.

So baptism is an outward sign of the working of the gospel. The gospel is the unlikely triumph of the surprising ways of God (i.e., the cross) over the predictably sinful ways of the world (i.e., power). The Corinthians had taken baptism, a sign of the humility of the cross, and turned it into a badge of pride and honor. The sign intended to unify had been co-opted by the pattern of the world and was now becoming a symbol of division. Ironic.

Paul is not knocking baptism; he is reordering the church's understanding of baptism in light of the gospel of Jesus Christ. Paul has come to preach the confoundingly humble and incomparably powerful gospel. We are about to witness this in a most stunning fashion. The gospel has a way of being unimpressively impressive, and Paul is about to demonstrate this for us. He will proclaim to us the ultimate oxymoron: the power of the cross.

There's name-dropping and then there's the "name above every name," which can't be dropped. Just try dropping Jesus' name at the next social gala and see how that goes.

The Prayer

Father, what is it in me that wants others to know who I know? Why do I try to make myself seem better or more important than I am? I confess, the patterns of the world run deep in me. And I am so tired of conforming to them. I long to be transformed by the renewing of my mind. Come, Holy Spirit, and lead me deeper into this way of the cross. I pray in Jesus' name, amen.

The Questions

- Though we live in a different cultural context, can you see these worldly ways of prestige- and status-seeking at work in the church today? What is it in us that clings to the ways of the world? What frightens us about the cross of Christ? Where are we clinging to worldly forms of power— The maintenance of our reputation? The preservation of our image? The status we gain from the people we know?

The Power of a Well-Placed Comma

4

1 CORINTHIANS 1:18–25 | For the message of the cross is foolishness to those who are perishing, but to us who are being saved it is the power of God. For it is written:

"I will destroy the wisdom of the wise;
the intelligence of the intelligent I will frustrate."

Where is the wise person? Where is the teacher of the law? Where is the philosopher of this age? Has not God made foolish the wisdom of the world? For since in the wisdom of God the world through its wisdom did not know him, God was pleased through the foolishness of what was preached to save those who believe. Jews demand signs and Greeks look for wisdom, but we preach Christ crucified: a stumbling block to Jews and foolishness to Gentiles, but to those whom God has called, both Jews and Greeks, Christ the power of God and the wisdom of God. For the foolishness of God is wiser than human wisdom, and the weakness of God is stronger than human strength.

Consider This

To those sanctified in Christ Jesus and called to be his holy people (i.e., us):

You know all too well the grammar joke about the panda who walks into a bar: He eats shoots and leaves. Now see how a well-placed comma completely changes the meaning: He eats, shoots, and leaves.

Where am I going with this? Thanks for asking. I remember years ago coming across an article written by Avery Cardinal Dulles in the esteemed journal *First Things*. He recounted being in a church and seeing a banner with the following words: "God is other people."

He desperately wanted to get out a marker and place a comma after the word "other," such that it would read: "God is other, people."

We will do well to recall those words we rehearsed yesterday from the prophet Isaiah.

> "For my thoughts are not your thoughts, neither are your ways my ways," declares the LORD.
>
> "As the heavens are higher than the earth, so are my ways higher than your ways and my thoughts than your thoughts." (Isa. 55:8–9)

Until we can come to terms with this basic tenet, we will have no hope of growing in the gospel. Today's text further amplifies this theme:

For the foolishness of God is wiser than human wisdom, and the weakness of God is stronger than human strength.

God is other, people. Paul's opening argument has everything to do with this comma. These Corinthian Christians were drifting away from the true and living God and moving toward the seduction of putting people in the place of God. Their faith had less and less to do with God and more and more to do with people. They were all about the pride of the human race and its intelligence, philosophies, philosophers, and teachers. It led to a situation antithetical to the gospel of Jesus Christ.

For the message of the cross is foolishness to those who are perishing, but to us who are being saved it is the power of God.

The confounding nature of the gospel is this: the God who is other became a person. This was and is pure foolishness in the eyes of the intelligentsia of every age. It is ridiculous, absurd, and downright foolishness that God would conde-scend to become an obscure Galilean peasant who would die the death of a heinous criminal and be resurrected from the dead.

we preach Christ crucified.

Paul is going to strip the gospel back to its pure essence, with no adornments or flourishes: Christ crucified. The message of the cross needs no help from people; only that they proclaim it. So what is the message of the cross? It can be described in so many ways. We could track out the Four Spiritual Laws or the Romans Road or powerful proof texts like "God was in Christ reconciling the world to himself, not counting peoples' sins against them" (2 Cor. 5:19) . . . all of which would be true and help us get at the truth, but how can we break it down into plain and simple language?

From the Scriptures through the early church and the church fathers, we see it expressed in a simplicity that is only exceeded by its profundity. It is this:

"God became like us so we could become like God."

God is other, people. But because God became a person, people can become like God.

This is the message of the cross. The way of the cross, then, is to repent and believe the gospel—over and over and over again. The power of the cross is that human beings, created in the image of God and broken by sin, can be saved from the penalty of sin, delivered from the power of sin, restored from the effects of sin, infused with the life of God through the person of the Holy Spirit, and transformed from one degree of glory to the next. In short, people can actually become like God, who is Jesus. It all comes back to our core calling to become a distinctively amazing kind of person.

The Prayer

Father God, thank you for the cross. And thank you for the message of the cross. It is so confounding and so right all at once. I can hardly comprehend it, and I suspect this is because it is revealed to the humble. I want to humble myself in your sight Lord. I ask you, by your Spirit, to reveal to my deepest mind and heart, the message of the cross. I renounce my foolishness. Count me in the number of those who are being saved. In Jesus' name, amen.

The Questions

- Do you believe this; that people can actually become like God (a.k.a. Jesus)? Have you come to terms with the nature of the foolishness of the cross as the power of God? How do you understand the cross as the foolishness of God?

The Problem with Beauty Pageants

5

1 CORINTHIANS 1:26–31 | Brothers and sisters, think of what you were when you were called. Not many of you were wise by human standards; not many were influential; not many were of noble birth. But God chose the foolish things of the world to shame the wise; God chose the weak things of the world to shame the strong. God chose the lowly things of this world and the despised things—and the things that are not—to nullify the things that are, so that no one may boast before him. It is because of him that you are in Christ Jesus, who has become for us wisdom from God—that is, our righteousness, holiness and redemption. Therefore, as it is written: "Let the one who boasts boast in the Lord."

Consider This

To those sanctified in Christ Jesus and called to be his holy people (i.e., us):

You've got to love Paul; what an apostolic straight shooter. He doesn't pull any punches.

Brothers and sisters, think of what you were when you were called. Not many of you were wise by human standards; not many were influential; not many were of noble birth.

Translation: You guys were riffraff. In fact, you still are. Redeemed riffraff. Highly cherished, valued, and even prized riffraff. Stop it! Stop trying to be like the culture around you.

Stop trying to imitate the so-called strong and so-called wise and so-called knowledgeable, intelligent people. Stop trying to be somebody and measure up in their world. God is doing something completely different with you—gloriously different. Later on, Paul will say things like, you are God's special field and you are God's building project.

God is not looking for the best and the brightest and most impressive people for his team. In fact, he's quite keen on picking the people who didn't get picked. Don't you love it when God sent Samuel to Jesse's house to anoint the next king of Israel. Jesse paraded his best, brightest, strongest, and most handsome sons before the prophet. I love what the Lord said to Samuel in the midst of this beauty pageant.

> But the LORD said to Samuel, "Do not consider his appearance or his height, for I have rejected him. The LORD does not look at the things people look at. People look at the outward appearance, but the LORD looks at the heart." (1 Sam. 16:7)

God chose David, the contestant who didn't even make the lineup. Samuel and Jesse and everybody else were caught up in the ways the world thinks. I am going to coin a phrase that might serve us for the next several weeks. Let's just call the ways the world evaluates people the "Corinthian categories." Now watch what God does with the Corinthian categories:

But God chose the foolish things of the world to shame the wise; God chose the weak things of the world to shame the strong. God chose the lowly things of this world and the despised things—and the things that are not—to nullify the things that are, so that no one may boast before him.

This makes the gospel very offensive. This is why it is very hard for a rich person to enter the kingdom of God. They have worked hard to build a kingdom on the categories of Corinth. There's too much to lose to let go of it. If only they could realize Jesus doesn't want their wealth. He wants them.

The gospel turns it all around. The kingdom of God is a turnaround kingdom. It upends Corinthian categories. It puts everyone on the same playing field. At the foot of the cross the ground is perfectly level. No one wins. No one loses. Jesus paid it all. The cross of Christ upends the categories of Corinth.

It is because of him that you are in Christ Jesus, who has become for us wisdom from God—that is, our righteousness, holiness and redemption.

Everyone belongs, and everything is beautiful. This is not utopian idealism. This is the eternal kingdom of Jesus Christ. Everyone experiences extraordinary blessing yet no one can boast.

These little churches Paul is planting across the first-century landscape are intended to be inordinately powerful demonstration plots of how the kingdom of God supplants and subverts the kingdoms of the world—how the cross of Christ obliterates the categories of Corinth.

The Prayer

Father, I dedicated so much time in my life to making myself in the image of the world, to trying to become important and valuable. Meanwhile, you upend this whole system by humbling yourself. It is hard to comprehend. Lay my heart bare before you. In Jesus' name, amen.

The Questions

- So how do you see the categories of Corinth at work in the church today? How is the church baptizing the ways of the world? How do you see the categories of Corinth at work in your life? How are you turning away from the patterns of this world and being transformed by the renewing of your mind? How is the message of the cross rooting out the ways of the world in your life? How will this word change your mentality today: "The LORD does not look at the things people look at. People look at the outward appearance, but the LORD looks at the heart" (1 Sam. 16:7)?

6 A Word to Preachers and the People Who Listen to Them

1 CORINTHIANS 2:1–5 ESV | And I, when I came to you, brothers, did not come proclaiming to you the testimony of God with lofty speech or wisdom. For I decided to know nothing among you except Jesus Christ and him crucified. And I was with you in weakness and in fear and much trembling, and my speech and my message were not in plausible words

of wisdom, but in demonstration of the Spirit and of power, so that your faith might not rest in the wisdom of men but in the power of God.

Consider This

To those sanctified in Christ Jesus and called to be his holy people (i.e., us):

Pop Quiz:

- People pick churches because of the _____.
- People evaluate churches based on the perceived effectiveness of the _____.
- People evaluate the Sunday worship service primarily according to what they thought about the

_____.

Okay, so here's how I filled in the blanks. Preacher. Preacher. Preacher. (We might insert "sermon" in that last blank but you get the point.) In short, the ability of the preacher has become the primary metric by which most people assess local churches. (In recent decades, music has become a very close second, and if the music is of a certain quality, people will even tolerate lower quality preaching.) We speak of great preachers and gifted preachers and amazing Bible teachers and such. At times, it rises to the level of "I follow Tim Keller," or "I follow Beth Moore," or "I follow John Piper," or "I follow (insert your own favorite preacher here)." It readily devolves into a cult of personality. When I served as a preacher in a large church years ago with multiple services and a variety of rotating preachers, people would call around the night before to try and determine which preacher would be in which service so they could plan accordingly. (I have a feeling that for me that selection process could go either way.)

What if instead of coming away from our church gatherings exclaiming to ourselves and others, "What an amazing preacher" or, "That was a great sermon," we said things like, "What an amazing God," or "That was a great demonstration of the gospel in the power of the Spirit"?

So what's a preacher to do? Should we try harder to be unimpressive or to be more average or what? No. I think Paul's point is to become a personal point of demonstration of the gospel being proclaimed. When God became a human person in Jesus Christ, the medium and the message become so inextricably bound together they could never be separated again. It's why Scripture says, "the Word became flesh and made his dwelling among us" (John 1:14).

Where the gospel is proclaimed with a demonstration of the Spirit's power, the attention of the people will be irresistibly drawn into an encounter with the living God rather than an assessment of the preacher or the message.

If the preacher is not himself or herself a demonstration of the foolishness of the cross, they may be communicating the truths of the gospel, but they are likely not proclaiming the gospel with a demonstration of the Spirit's power. It is not a preacher's job to convince people of the truth of the gospel. The preacher's calling is to become a living, breathing demonstration of the message of the cross in the pulpit and, more importantly, out of the pulpit.

If I am even remotely similar to the majority of the preachers of this day and time, I would assess our major problem as being far more concerned with our delivery of the message than we are about a demonstration of the Spirit's power. Sure, we want a demonstration of the Spirit's power but we readily confuse this with a demonstration of our own polished skills.

(And the truth of the matter—because most of us are not capable of highly polished oratory—is that we allow ourselves to slip into the easy mediocrity of preparing neither the message nor the messenger, instead serving God's people warmed-over sermons salted with sentiment and peppered with humor.)

In order to proclaim the gospel, which is the message of the cross, we must learn to err on the side of emphasizing the preparation of the messenger rather than on the preparation of the message. While I do not want to set up a false dichotomy here, a distinction must be made.

Here's some good news for the rest of us: the proclamation of the gospel is simply not the domain of the great communicators. It is the humble privilege of broken men and women who are themselves being daily remade by the message of the foolishness of the cross.

The Prayer

Father, thank you for the gift of preaching and the gift of preachers, but thank you more for a demonstration of the

Spirit's power through the proclamation of Christ crucified. I want to pray for preachers everywhere today and especially the preacher who regularly proclaims the Word of God in my church. Bless him or her with a deepened anointing. Lead them to embrace the foolishness of the cross and bring a demonstration of the Spirit's power through their ministry. Help me to become a better hearer too. I pray in Jesus' name, amen.

The Questions

• To preachers: Where do you push back on today's entry? Why? How do you resonate with it? What will you do next? To people who listen to preachers: What role do you play on the demand side of wanting to hear awesome preachers? What metrics do you use to assess great preachers/great messages? To preachers and the people who listen to them: What would a demonstration of the Spirit's power look like? What's the difference between the foolishness of a preacher and the foolishness of the cross?

7 The Real Meaning of Maturity

1 CORINTHIANS 2:6–10 | We do, however, speak a message of wisdom among the mature, but not the wisdom of this age or of the rulers of this age, who are coming to nothing. No, we declare God's wisdom, a mystery that has been hidden and that God destined for our glory before time began. None of the rulers of this age understood it, for if they had, they would not have crucified the Lord of glory. However, as it is written:

"What no eye has seen,
   what no ear has heard,
and what no human mind has conceived"—
   the things God has prepared for those who love him—

these are the things God has revealed to us by his Spirit.

Consider This

To those sanctified in Christ Jesus and called to be his holy people (i.e., us):

Knowledge, insight, understanding, and gifts have a way of creating detours for the followers of Jesus. Paul is drawing another sharp contrast for the Corinthians between the categories of Corinth and the ways of the kingdom of God. The new Christians in Corinth were having a difficult time leaving behind the old ways of being a Corinthian. Instead, as invariably happens, they were overlaying their old, dead understandings onto the new and living way of the cross.

In the old system, leaders and the people who followed them distinguished themselves by their sophisticated knowledge of wisdom. The most knowledgeable, insightful, eloquent, and impressive won the day. It produced a sort of classism, which created all sorts of distinctions and divisions among people. The Corinthians naturally brought this same value system right into their church with all its elitist, egotistical baggage.

Here's the big irony: they considered that Paul was giving them milk. They wanted to get on to the deeper stuff, the real wisdom. You know, the stuff that would make them smarter, better, and more mature than those other people. "Where's the beef?" they seemed to be asking. Paul was actually giving them the beef. He was giving them the straight-up truth of the gospel, which completely undermined their old ways of relating to each other. Whereas before they were all looking for a way to distinguish themselves as the more knowledgeable, insightful, and mature ones, Paul told them the truth . . . which was precisely the opposite. The cross crushes all such class distinctions. There were no special classes of Christians. In fact, the mark of a Christian was they would not only consider one another as equals, they would consider one another as better than themselves.

Through the life, death, resurrection, and ascension of Jesus and the coming of the Holy Spirit, a new day had come and the old system had been given notice. Those ways were coming to nothing. The way long hidden—the mystery—was no longer a secret. It was public knowledge. There was a catch though. The mystery of the message of the cross is the way it is hidden from the proud yet revealed to the humble. It was not a source of knowledge or wisdom that could be seized or taken control of or manipulated. Didn't Jesus pray something strangely familiar?

> At that time Jesus said, "I praise you, Father, Lord of heaven and earth, because you have hidden these things from the wise and learned, and revealed them to little children. Yes, Father, for this is what you were pleased to do." (Matt. 11:25–26)

This wisdom of God could only be received as a gift through the humility of bowing at the foot of the cross, on the level ground at the feet of Jesus. And I think this is precisely the message—the truly solid food these Corinthians mistook for milk. The maturity of a person's faith in Jesus is precisely commensurate with their growth in humility.

Right there—at the foot of the cross, at the feet of Jesus—all of the revelation of God is made known to anyone who would get close enough to the ground to receive it.

"What no eye has seen, what no ear has heard, and what no human mind has conceived"—the things God has prepared for those who love him—these are the things God has revealed to us by his Spirit.

These Corinthian Christians wanted to be just that—Corinthian Christians. They wanted to import the gospel into their already existing framework of power structures and social norms. The message of the cross would transform them into Christian Corinthians. See the difference?

The Prayer

Father in heaven, thank you for bringing your glory to earth in the form of the humble one—your Son, Jesus Christ. What a marvel it is to behold him in all of his humble glory, and what a miracle it is that you can make us like him. Lord, I want to be humble. So much stands in the way. Come, Holy Spirit, and cause my eyes to see and my ears to hear and my mind to conceive and my heart to turn fully to you that I might know what you have prepared for me. I do love you, Lord. In Jesus' name, amen.

The Questions

- What part of the old value system of the world do you find the hardest to leave behind? It's likely that part of it that you most built your life and identity around. What would that be for you? Prestige, wealth, appearance, possessions, respectability, position, status? What, for you, might be the difference between an American Christian and a Christian American? Have you experienced elitist Christians— people who claim special status or secret revelation from God? Have you ever been one of those people? How do you resonate with this definition of maturity and its relationship to humility?

8 Why I'm Not a Disciple-Maker and You Aren't Either

1 CORINTHIANS 2:10–16 | The Spirit searches all things, even the deep things of God. For who knows a person's

thoughts except their own spirit within them? In the same way no one knows the thoughts of God except the Spirit of God. What we have received is not the spirit of the world, but the Spirit who is from God, so that we may understand what God has freely given us. This is what we speak, not in words taught us by human wisdom but in words taught by the Spirit, explaining spiritual realities with Spirit-taught words. The person without the Spirit does not accept the things that come from the Spirit of God but considers them foolishness, and cannot understand them because they are discerned only through the Spirit. The person with the Spirit makes judgments about all things, but such a person is not subject to merely human judgments, for,

"Who has known the mind of the Lord
so as to instruct him?"

But we have the mind of Christ.

Consider This

To those sanctified in Christ Jesus and called to be his holy people (i.e., us):

Paul is the consummate disciple-maker. These Corinthian Christians have gotten off track. Word gets back to Paul. He writes them letters. In this letter, Paul ever so diplomatically and gently takes them back to square one—the cross of Jesus Christ or "Christ crucified" as Paul put it. From there he goes to square two, retraining them in the ways of the person and work of the Holy Spirit.

And what is the Holy Spirit up to? He reveals, reorients, and renews our minds according to the mind of Christ.

Discipleship is the supernatural process of a human person being remade in the image of God, which means being re-formed in the mind of Christ. We are not the disciple-makers. The Holy Spirit is the disciple-maker. We participate with the Holy Spirit's work in the Holy Spirit's ways in the midst of the community fellowship the Holy Spirit creates to restore our broken race into the radiant beauty of God's glory. That's what discipleship is all about.

I want you to notice the powerful pneumatology ($25 seminary word meaning, in essence, a theology of the Spirit) in Paul's words:

This is what we speak, not in words taught us by human wisdom but in words taught by the Spirit, explaining spiritual realities with Spirit-taught words.

Discipleship is not the wise teaching the unwise. It is not the mature teaching the immature. It is not the professionals teaching the amateurs. In fact, discipleship does not happen in power-oriented relationships or in social contexts built on status-oriented relationships. True Christian discipleship only happens in the midst of a community of people who prefer one another over themselves and who together learn to love one another with the very essence of the supernatural holy love of God (see also 1 Corinthians 13).

Just because we call whatever it is we are doing in the church "discipleship" does not make it discipleship. Discipleship cannot be reduced to a program or a formula or a plan or a curriculum. The mind of Christ, the life of Jesus—which is itself the message of the cross—is our curriculum.

It's why Paul, writing to the Christian Philippians, put it this way:

> In your relationships with one another, have the same mindset as Christ Jesus: Who, being in very nature God, did not consider equality with God something to be used to his own advantage; rather, he made himself nothing by taking the very nature of a servant, being made in human likeness. And being found in appearance as a man, he humbled himself by becoming obedient to death—even death on a cross!
>
> Therefore God exalted him to the highest place and gave him the name that is above every name, that at the name of Jesus every knee should bow, in heaven and on earth and under the earth, and every tongue acknowledge that Jesus Christ is Lord, to the glory of God the Father. (Phil. 2:5–11)

The Holy Spirit is the teacher who makes us disciples together in the community of the humble where the would-be disciple-maker and the disciple cannot be distinguished from one another. Picture Jesus washing his disciples' feet and you have it.

It's why Paul, writing to the Christian Romans, put it this way, "Do not be conformed any longer to the pattern of this world, but be transformed by the renewing of your mind" (Rom. 12:2).

When we look back on our lives, we will realize it was the most humble, unassuming believers who the Holy Spirit most employed in making us disciples of Jesus Christ. They probably weren't even trying to disciple us. Through the sheer unadulterated authenticity of their faith-full lives the Holy Spirit discipled us. Let us aspire to become those kinds of people today—for the sake of others.

The Prayer

Father, thank you for the people who have discipled me, the ones who knew they were doing it and the ones who did it unawares. Let it be so between me and others. Come, Holy Spirit, and form in me the mind of Christ that I might become who Jesus would be if he were me. I pray in Jesus' name, amen.

The Questions

- What do you think of this notion of the Holy Spirit being the disciple-maker? How does that change the way we think about our role in the process? Where are you challenged by today's text and reflection? Where do you push back on this way of framing it? What insights might the Holy Spirit be impressing on you now? What are the implications of those for today?

The Problem of Worldly Christians and the Remedy

9

1 CORINTHIANS 3:1–4 | Brothers and sisters, I could not address you as people who live by the Spirit but as people who are still worldly—mere infants in Christ. I gave you milk, not solid food, for you were not yet ready for it. Indeed, you are still not ready. You are still worldly. For since there is jealousy and quarreling among you, are you not worldly? Are you not acting like mere humans? For when one says, "I follow Paul," and another, "I follow Apollos," are you not mere human beings?

Consider This

To those sanctified in Christ Jesus and called to be his holy people (i.e., us):

Perhaps one of the great oxymorons in the Bible would be the combination of the two words "worldly Christian," yet this is precisely Paul's assessment of the Corinthian Christians. There are new Christians, and then there are immature Christians, and they aren't the same thing. An immature Christian is one who has become stunted in their growth or arrested in development. The goal of discipleship—which is the work of the Holy Spirit to restore a human person to the image of God and the mind of Christ—is to bring forth mature adult Christians. Nothing stunts the growth or arrests the development of a person's or a community's faith like worldliness does.

So what does it mean to be a worldly Christian? A worldly Christian is a person who cannot leave behind the patterns of the world. They are neither hot nor cold but lukewarm. They are neither yes nor no but are always, "it depends." A worldly Christian is a person who has become ensnared by the seductive strategies of the unholy trinity: money, sex, and power.

So what is the opposite of worldliness? We might describe it as godliness or holiness or Christlikeness or glorious or even beautiful. All of these are ways of describing what it means to be spiritual. To be spiritual, in the biblical sense, means to be inspired and animated at the core of one's being by the indwelling Holy Spirit. To be spiritual means to belong to God in such a way that one's very character and essence increasingly resembles the character and nature of God.

Becoming a mature follower of Jesus Christ necessarily means leaving behind worldliness without leaving behind the world. This is the point where so much of the Christianity of our time gets off the rails.

You are still worldly. For since there is jealousy and quarreling among you, are you not worldly? Are you not acting like mere humans?

Worldliness smacks of pride. The crazy thing about worldly Christians is they usually have no idea of it.

All of this brings to mind Jesus' parable of the sower. My sense is that Paul is drawing from this teaching as he works with the Corinthian church. "Still others, like seed sown among thorns, hear the word; but the worries of this life, the deceitfulness of wealth and the desires for other things come in and choke the word, making it unfruitful" (Mark 4:18–19).

The Prayer

Our Father in heaven, thank you for the hard word from your Word about growing up into a mature follower of your Son, Jesus. Please show me where I am yet immature. Expose my worldliness. I do not want to conform to the patterns of this world, yet some of those run so deep in me I have no idea of it. Search me, Holy Spirit. Ferret out those offensive ways and lead me in the way of Jesus. In his name I pray, amen.

The Questions

- Let's do a scaling exercise. On a scale of 1–10 with 1 representing worldly and 10 representing spiritual, where would you place yourself? Can you think of a person you consider to be an authentically spiritual person in the way Paul talks about? Where do you most struggle with worldliness? What would it look like to become less worldly and more spiritual?

10 | What Farmers Know That the Rest of Us Don't

1 CORINTHIANS 3:5–8 ESV | What then is Apollos? What is Paul? Servants through whom you believed, as the Lord assigned to each. I planted, Apollos watered, but God gave the growth. So neither he who plants nor he who waters is anything, but only God who gives the growth. He who plants and he who waters are one, and each will receive his wages according to his labor.

Consider This

To those sanctified in Christ Jesus and called to be his holy people (i.e., us):

Aristotle once said, "The soul never thinks without a picture."

The writers of Scripture seemed to know this intuitively. "Jesus spoke all these things to the crowd in parables; he did not say anything to them without using a parable" (Matt. 13:34).

The Word of God and the Spirit of God are always conspiring to open the eyes of our hearts. The goal of any disciple-maker worth their salt is not to increase our store of information but to cause our souls to think. Paul is no exception. In fact, he is a master. Paul has laid aside any need to impress anyone with impressive speech and "resolved to know nothing while I was with you except Jesus Christ and him crucified" (1 Cor. 2:2).

Everything he says and does, every metaphor he employs, every picture he paints, are all aimed to this singular purpose.

Paul chooses the most ancient metaphor of them all in today's text: farming. If there's one thing farmers know perhaps better than the rest of us, it is that farmers must simultaneously work tirelessly and depend completely. In the end, a true farmer can take credit for hard work and wise decision making, but everyone knows they made nothing grow. The miracle of a seed's germination, its gravity-defying growth, its maturation into a plant, and miraculous multiplication into many seeds—this is the doing of God. It's why farmers, of all people, don't tend to be boastful.

While this metaphor is pregnant with all sorts of meaning and insight, Paul's application is clear. The ministry of the gospel is not about the farmers; it's about God.

I planted, Apollos watered, but God gave the growth. So neither he who plants nor he who waters is anything, but only God who gives the growth.

The workers will be rewarded, and one of the greatest rewards of all is the sheer joy of getting to be a part of it all. The message of Christ crucified keeps everything in perspective.

What we most need in the season ahead are gospel movements not built around personalities. It's easy to blame Apollos, but Paul will not do it. He puts the fault at the feet of the Corinthians for elevating leaders to a kind of celebrity status and then wrapping themselves in the prestige of the one they follow. This is the worldliness Paul eschews because of the way it creates divisive cults of personality and caricatures of the church rather than authentic movements of the gospel that level the playing field and glorify God alone.

The Prayer

Our Father in heaven, thank you for your Word—for the way you sow your Word in my heart and then by your Spirit cause it to grow. Thank you that you have the patience of a farmer, who will sow and wait and even reseed the ground of my soul. Cultivate my life into a fruitful harvest. Come, Holy Spirit, and break up my fallow ground, make my life a demonstration plot of the goodness and grace of Jesus Christ. In his name, I pray. Amen.

The Questions

- How does Paul's farming metaphor cause your soul to think? What does it mean to play your role and yet depend completely on God? How do we honor our leaders without putting them on a pedestal? What would it mean for you to be a servant through whom someone else came to believe?

11 On Christ the Solid Rock I Stand?

1 CORINTHIANS 3:9–15 | For we are co-workers in God's service; you are God's field, God's building.

By the grace God has given me, I laid a foundation as a wise builder, and someone else is building on it. But each one should build with care. For no one can lay any foundation other than the one already laid, which is Jesus Christ. If anyone builds on this foundation using gold, silver, costly stones, wood, hay or straw, their work will be shown for what it is, because the Day will bring it to light. It will be revealed with fire, and the fire will test the quality of each person's work. If what has been built survives, the builder will receive a reward. If it is burned up, the builder will suffer loss but yet will be saved—even though only as one escaping through the flames.

Consider This

To those sanctified in Christ Jesus and called to be his holy people (i.e., us):

In the founding documents of Harvard University, we find the following paragraph:

> Let every Student be plainly instructed, and earnestly pressed to consider well, the main end of his life and studies is, to know God and Jesus Christ which is eternal life (John 17:3) and therefore to lay Christ in the bottom, as the only foundation of all sound knowledge and Learning. And seeing the Lord only giveth wisdom, Let every one seriously set himself by prayer in secret to seek it of him. (Prov. 2:3)

To lay Christ in the bottom . . . it's a word about the foundation. The big problem though was the way they proceeded over the ensuing centuries to build on top of the foundation. Somewhere along the way, they started building with materials that bore little resemblance to the stated foundation. The irony is, today Harvard is considered the gold standard of higher education. I'll leave it there.

The foundation matters most. If the foundation is corrupt, everything built on top of it is also corrupted. Remember Jesus' prescient words,

> "Therefore everyone who hears these words of mine and puts them into practice is like a wise man who built his house on the rock. The rain came down, the streams rose, and the winds blew and beat against that house; yet it did not fall, because it had its foundation on the rock. But everyone who hears these words of mine and does not put them into practice is like a foolish man who built his house on sand. The rain came down, the streams rose, and the winds blew and beat against that house, and it fell with a great crash." (Matt. 7:24–27)

While the foundation is critical, it's hardly all that matters. It's not enough to have a solid foundation. The rest of the structure must be built on the same quality materials. The building materials must be worthy of the foundation.

In this instance, Paul is clear that he laid the solid foundation of Christ crucified. His concern is about those who have come after him building with shoddy materials. Perhaps it was this worldly wisdom he was referring to. Maybe it was false teaching altogether. Whatever it was, Paul clearly indicated that it may take years for the flaws to present themselves, but they could be sure their work would be tested.

What about today? How are we to understand this text? We might think about our children and the kind of foundation being laid for them. Are they being raised to stand on the unshakable gospel of Jesus Christ or on the shifting sands of the seductive culture around us? How are we building on that foundation? Are we training them up in the strength of the Word and the security of the Holy Spirit? How about our churches? Are we building real Christians or are we content to assume everybody has their ticket punched and is okay?

I think this is precisely the cancerous epidemic in the American church. We are fairly competent at letting people know they need to have a personal relationship with Jesus in order to go to heaven when they die, but we seem pretty content to leave it there. What about the rest of the gospel? There's *justification by grace through faith*: the foundation. Then there's *sanctification by grace through faith*: the building on top of the foundation. The New Testament makes a clarion call to the second half of the gospel at every turn.

> And we all, who with unveiled faces contemplate the Lord's glory, are being transformed into his image with ever-increasing glory, which comes from the Lord, who is the Spirit. (2 Cor. 3:18)

> So then, just as you received Christ Jesus as Lord, continue to live your lives in him, rooted and built up in him, strengthened in the faith as you were taught, and overflowing with thankfulness. (Col. 2:6–7)

> His divine power has given us everything we need for a godly life through our knowledge of him who called us by his own glory and goodness. Through these he has given us his very great and precious promises, so that through them you may participate in the divine nature, having escaped the corruption in the world caused by evil desires. (2 Peter 1:3–4)

I could go on. I think you see my point. It's time to get on with the gospel. At Seedbed, we call it the "second half of the gospel." The world around us will believe the first half of the gospel when the people of God wake up to the second half of the gospel. It's time to build with gold and silver and costly stones. Our work will be tested. In fact, it is already being tested in us every single day.

The Prayer

Father, thank you for all the ways the foundation of Jesus Christ was built into my life. Thank you for all the ways my family and other people have built into my life with gold, silver, and costly stones. Show me this way of investing in others and building into their lives. Come, Holy Spirit, and lead me into the kind of transformation of which only you are capable. Let me settle for nothing less. In Jesus' name, amen.

The Questions

- How about the foundation on which your life and faith are built? Are you securely planted on the grace of the gospel of Jesus Christ who gave his life for you while you were a sinner? Are you attempting to stand on your own merits in any way, shape, or form? How about your own growth in the gospel? What is the shape of the gospel building project of your life? Where might you be arrested in development? What kind of materials are you using to build on the foundation of Jesus Christ in your family? With people you are leading in discipleship in one form or another? Have you accepted this call to be a co-laborer with God—a builder of kingdom quality into the lives of others?

Why Your Local Church Matters and Why It Might Not

12

1 CORINTHIANS 3:16–17 ESV | Do you not know that you are God's temple and that God's Spirit dwells in you? If anyone destroys God's temple, God will destroy him. For God's temple is holy, and you are that temple.

Consider This

To those sanctified in Christ Jesus and called to be his holy people (i.e., us):

Later in the letter we will see Paul reference a human person's physical body as a "temple of God." Through the centuries, many have made the mistake of reading this text in light of this later one, which has led to missing the essential meaning of verses 16–17. In other words, while the reference in chapter 6 is clearly about an individual's physical body, today's text is about something much larger: the local church.

We so readily read the Bible as though it were written to us as individuals. While there is much to be said about individual application, the Bible, for the most part, is speaking to us as a people—God's holy people. Being an individualistic society, we see the personal pronoun "you" as meaning "me" when most of the time in Scripture the "you" should be interpreted as "us." This does not diminish the individual in the least. If anything, it creates a context of loving accountability for the individual to actually become a real Christian and not just an outwardly religious one.

John Wesley once famously said something to the effect of, "There is no holiness apart from social holiness." This gets routinely misinterpreted as having something to do with social justice. While Wesley was all for social justice, this is not what he meant. His point is that it is impossible to become holy alone. Becoming holy only happens in a community of people actively participating in the Holy Spirit's sanctifying work among them. While a person can only be justified before God alone, as an individual, people can only be sanctified, or made holy, together—in the midst of a community. The people together are the temple of God.

God's Spirit tabernacles in the midst of God's people—not apart from the world but right in the midst of the world.

This calling to be God's holy people—which you will remember is the banner we are stretching across every page—is not a calling to offer an alternative religion to the larger community but an alternative demonstration of the good and true and beautiful life of the living God unleashed in the world.

One of the consistent bottom lines running through all of Paul's communications to local churches—and this one chief among them—is this calling to become a dramatically different kind of community than the surrounding culture.

When Paul says, "Do you not know" (and he says it no less than ten times in this letter), he's in effect saying, "Wake up, people! You are God's alternative offer in the midst of this lost world. The Holy Spirit dwells in your midst! You are the church in this city! You are the Corinthians' last and best hope. Humble yourselves now that you may rise up into the lives for which you were made."

The truth? He's saying that to our local churches today. What if we really heard this? I suspect that the extent to which a local church becomes deeply aware of God's Spirit dwelling in their midst is the difference between being a local church that matters and one that does not.

The Prayer

Our Father, thank you for the way you make me a temple of the Holy Spirit. And thank you for the way you make us together the temple of the Holy Spirit in the midst of this world. I confess I am stuck in my own brokenness apart from relationships with others, yet by your Spirit in the midst of relationships with others I am being made holy. Come, Holy Spirit, and lead me deeper into the kind of community where you can make me a gift to others and others a gift to me. In Jesus' name, amen.

The Questions

• What would it mean for your local church to be so alive in the Holy Spirit who is in your midst that it became a beautiful thing to the surrounding community? How is this happening in your church? What would need to change for this to happen? What is the level of awareness among your community of believers of this reality: "The Holy Spirit dwells in your midst." How could that awareness grow? What are the implications of this awareness not growing? (Resist the temptation to blame the lack of awareness on the church's leaders.)

13 When the Church Should Divide and When It Shouldn't

1 CORINTHIANS 3:18–23 | Do not deceive yourselves. If any of you think you are wise by the standards of this age, you should become "fools" so that you may become wise. For the wisdom of this world is foolishness in God's sight. As it is written: "He catches the wise in their craftiness"; and again, "The Lord knows that the thoughts of the wise are futile." So then, no more boasting about human leaders! All things are yours, whether Paul or Apollos or Cephas or the world or life or death or the present or the future—all are yours, and you are of Christ, and Christ is of God.

Consider This

To those sanctified in Christ Jesus and called to be his holy people (i.e., us):

I'm a Methodist! I'm a Baptist! I'm a Roman Catholic! I'm a Pentecostal! I'm an Anglican! I follow Wesley! I follow Calvin! I follow Arminius! I follow Luther! And on we go.

Could Paul possibly be addressing us as we read over the shoulders of the Corinthian church? I don't want to make a sweeping and overly simplistic analogy and application here, but I think it bears some consideration. In this letter, Paul is chiding the Corinthians for dividing themselves up and opposing one another based on the particular leader they associated with. All of them were seeking to get a leg up on wisdom and knowledge in ways that would make them superior to one another. They were importing this mentality of a superior position based on the superior teaching of their particular teacher or spokesperson. This was exactly how they operated in the world in their pursuit of *sophia*, or "worldly wisdom," before they became followers of Jesus.

They brought this same approach right into the way they approached the gospel. I don't so much think we are dealing with the issue of false teaching at this point in the letter as we are dealing with a divisive and thereby destructive way of approaching the gospel.

In a sense, each of these groups were claiming a superior brand of the truth over and against the others. How is this different from the way the church (notably the Protestant church) has operated for the past five hundred years? I think we are somewhere north of twenty thousand different denominations or distinctive groups across the body of Christ in 2020. Now, resist the temptation to interpret me as saying something I am not saying. I do not mean to say we should all uniformly agree on every point of doctrine and teaching and such. There are essentials that comprise the orthodox Christian faith, and there are a variety of matters on which we can respectfully differ without divisiveness. In fact, these ways in which we differ often amount to things we emphasize more than others and can hold the potential to become greater complementary gifts to each other.

For instance, the Calvinists bring us a focused vision of the glorious sovereignty and kingship of God in all things while the Wesleyans bring into focus the character of God's sovereignty through the lens of the fatherhood of God. We could go on with this kind of complementary distinctiveness ad infinitum, and it would be a very profitable exercise.

Do we differ to the degree of holding some serious arguments? Absolutely! But we need not divide over it and attempt to distinguish our superior version over and against each other. Is division then always wrong? By no means!

Permit me what may be perceived as a digression by some but to others will be understood as a word fitly spoken for the times in which we live. When one group among us decides to depart from the essential orthodoxy of the Christian faith or they take positions which erode and undermine essentials like the authority of Scripture or the uniqueness of Jesus Christ and his life, death, and resurrection, we need not so much decide to divide as we need to discern that division has happened. It can either be reconciled or the divided parties must go their respective ways and get on with being the church and proclaiming the gospel as they understand it—with the confidence that we can all entrust ourselves to the one who judges justly and his ultimate resolution, which we may or may not see in our lifetime.

At times in the history of the church such matters have taken centuries to sort out. In these rare cases where a house is divided over matters of core orthodoxy, it simply cannot stand. It will implode under the weight of its own conflict. The appeal for unity at all costs in the face of actual division over orthodoxy can itself become a type of heresy, which destroys the church from within. And, to be clear, it will not destroy the church (which is indestructible), but it will devastate people by the force of unwitting deception and lead to broken lives and the shipwrecking of priceless faith on the shoals of the spirit of our times.

Back to the primary point at hand: Let's follow our Wesleys and Calvins and Cranmers and so forth as our spirit resonates with their teaching and vision for the advance of the gospel, but let's avoid distinguishing and dividing ourselves over and against one another according to who we follow. Hear Paul clearly on this point:

So then, no more boasting about human leaders! All things are yours, whether Paul or Apollos or Cephas or the world or life or death or the present or the future—all are yours, and you are of Christ, and Christ is of God.

What if we looked upon all these traditions and leaders as belonging to all of us in the sense that we all bring particular gifts that can enrich the others, help us see our blind spots, and cause us to temper our overstated strengths and to be shored up in our under-recognized weaknesses? The kingdom of God does not grow by conformity but through a unified and celebrated diversity.

All of these are ours, and we are of Christ and Christ is of God!

Glory be to the Father, and to the Son, and to the Holy Spirit. As it was in the beginning, is now, and ever shall be. World without end, amen.

The Prayer

Our Father in heaven, thank you for the gift of the church, the body of Christ. Thank you that the church's one foundation is Jesus Christ our Lord. Give us the courage to recognize when our differences threaten to compromise this foundation. Otherwise, forgive us for the way we allow differences to divide us. Come, Holy Spirit, and give us the gift of a gentle yet unwavering conviction on all things essential, a generous posture toward one another on all matters non-essential, and a penetrating and incisive wisdom to discern the difference. We pray in Jesus' name, amen.

The Questions

- Have you or the part of the church with which you most align distinguished yourselves by deprecating the parts of the church with which you have disagreement? Have you tended to follow a particular leader (e.g., Wesley) while disparaging another (e.g., Calvin)? What might repentance look like for you? What would it mean to follow your particular leader without boasting in them? What gifts do you see in receiving the influence of teachers and movements which you have not heretofore given credence or pride of place? What can we learn from the Pentecostals? From the Calvinists? From the Mennonites? From the Wesleyans? What are we afraid of or what keeps us from opening ourselves up to these influences? From recognizing we are playing on the same team?

14 Working at the Bottom of the Org Chart While Reporting to the Top

1 CORINTHIANS 4:1–5 ESV | This, then, is how you ought to regard us: as servants of Christ and as those entrusted with the mysteries God has revealed. Now it is required that those who have been given a trust must prove faithful. I care very little if I am judged by you or by any human court; indeed, I do not even judge myself. My conscience is clear, but that does not make me innocent. It is the Lord who judges me. Therefore judge nothing before the appointed time; wait until the Lord comes. He will bring to light what is hidden in darkness and will expose the motives of the heart. At that time each will receive their praise from God.

Consider This

To those sanctified in Christ Jesus and called to be his holy people (i.e., us):

If there is one thing Paul is clear about, it is his place in the world. He knows where he stands in the org chart. And where is that? He is at the bottom, below everyone else. Paul is a servant. There is a twist though. Though Paul is at the bottom of the org chart, below everyone else in status and rank, he has a direct reporting relationship to God himself. Paul knows himself as a beloved son of a perfect Father. Paul has been entrusted to serve and steward the household of God. He all at once holds the lowest rank yet reports to the highest authority. That's pretty interesting. In case we need more assurance on this point, remember earlier how Paul likened himself and his co-laborers to farm workers and then to construction workers.

Consider the largest company you can think of and imagine the janitorial custodian reporting directly to the CEO, and we get close to Paul's point. Paul is not beholden to middle management. He is not flippant or arrogant about that, because he knows he will ultimately be judged by God—which will include an assessment of how he treated everyone in the entire organization. Our calling is to blue collar, ground-level servanthood to other people—even if we happen to find ourselves wearing a white collar and sitting in a corner office on the twenty-fourth floor.

It brings to mind one of the most pivotal scenes in human history.

> Jesus knew that the Father had put all things under his power, and that he had come from God and was returning to God; so he got up from the meal, took off his outer clothing, and wrapped a towel around his waist. After that, he poured water into a basin and began to wash his disciples' feet, drying them with the towel that was wrapped around him. (John 13:3–5)

Discipleship in the way of Jesus means developing a deeply held humble self-understanding of our identity as the beloved sons and daughters of a perfect Father. Those first clauses of the passage may be the most important. "Jesus knew that the Father had put all things under his power, and that he had come from God and was returning to God."

When a person properly understands their identity in relationship to God, they are set free to serve others without regard for themselves. They can do the most menial task or the most exalted work without preferring one to the other. Nothing is above us or beneath us to do in the service of others. It's interesting to note what happens just after the foot washing is the Lord's Supper—moving from the most humble moment to the most divine, in the span of an evening.

Our big problem is the way we confuse our identity with our role, mistaking our worth as a person with our performance of a job. When our identity is linked up with our performance, our performance becomes a way of validating ourselves—which makes everything we do, no matter how apparently noble it may be, a backdoor way of serving ourselves. This is the essence of slavery to self.

We are no longer slaves to fear, but children of the Most High God. It's a declaration of identity. Freedom only comes from the ever-deepening gift of an identity anchored in the holy love of the God and Father of our Lord Jesus Christ. Everything else is the futile effort of an insecure slave trying to hammer out their worth on the anvil of somebody else's opinion of them.

There's a massive difference in doing service-oriented things and taking on the nature of a servant. It's only when we can walk away from every other source of worth and stake our identity solely and securely on the nature God bestows upon us as his sons and daughters—only then are we free to take on the nature of a servant (see Philippians 2:5–11).

The Prayer

Our Father in heaven, we marvel at the amazing grace you have shown us in your Son Jesus Christ. Lead me to share in the very nature of his relationship with you; to know your deep and abiding love for myself, just as I am, apart from anything I have done or failed to do; to know the favor of a son or daughter. Come, Holy Spirit, and heal the brokenness in my core identity and lead me into a way of serving you and others from that core wellness. I pray in Jesus' name, amen.

The Questions

- Is your Christian discipleship staying in the shallow end of doing service-oriented things or are you launching out into the depths of knowing your identity in Jesus Christ, where you can truly take on the nature of a servant?

Why I Think I'm Better than You and Why It Must Stop

15

1 CORINTHIANS 4:6–7 | Now, brothers and sisters, I have applied these things to myself and Apollos for your benefit, so that you may learn from us the meaning of the saying, "Do not go beyond what is written." Then you will not be puffed up in being a follower of one of us over against the other. For who makes you different from anyone else? What do you have that you did not receive? And if you did receive it, why do you boast as though you did not?

Consider This

To those sanctified in Christ Jesus and called to be his holy people (i.e., us):

One of the hardest things about becoming a real Christian and growing in the grace of God is becoming "crucified to the world." It means laying aside every distinction we have earned or added to our résumés in order to become just like everyone else. Am I speaking of some kind of chosen mediocrity? No! I am speaking of authentic humility, which is a proper estimation of ourselves as men and women who stand before God with nothing in our hands.

Everyone has had the experience of being in the labor and delivery ward of a hospital and gazing through the glass at the freshly born group of babies. In some ways they all look the same, yet all of them are gloriously distinctive. We never look in on the group and consider that one child is more valuable than another unless one of those children belongs to us. Still, this child of ours is distinguished by nothing else other than our particular affection for him or her. Even in our affection, we still do not somehow consider our child as better than the other precious surrounding newborns.

This begins to change the minute these children leave the hospital and enter into the world with all its distorted economies of class, privilege, and poverty. From this moment forward, the parents, and later the children themselves, will give themselves to distinguishing their child as more intelligent, better dressed, more gifted, more schooled, more skilled, more privileged, more athletic, more connected to more important people, and, yes, more valuable than the kids down the street or across the country.

I've got good news and bad news for us. The bad news? The cross of Jesus Christ crushes this entire value system. The good news? The cross of Jesus Christ crushes this entire value system. Here's the rub though. We unwittingly bring this entire value system with us into the church and even into our relationship with God. From the beauty of our baptismal gowns to our country club confirmation celebrations, we press right on with the system. We've all seen the T-shirts: "God loves you, but I'm his favorite." There's tongue-in-cheek truth in it, but truth no less.

The Baptists are more saved than the Methodists. The Pentecostals are more spiritual than the Baptists. The Bible Church people are more biblical than the rest of us, and the Church of Christ people . . . they're going to be the only ones who make it to heaven anyway. It's not a perfect analogy to today's text but it gets at the point. This entire system might fairly be called the power of pride or equally, the pride of power. We take pride in our distinctions to the point of dividing over them, even if we keep up the show of sticking together.

*For who makes you different from anyone else? What do you
have that you did not receive? And if you did receive it, why do
you boast as though you did not?*

Baptism in the name of the triune God takes us right back
into that hospital labor and delivery nursery. It's why one of
the ways the Bible refers to salvation is being born again. All
our worldly distinctions, all our merit badges, are stripped
of their power to bolster our identity and inflate our importance. Once again, we are all the same. We are given another
chance to embrace the humility of our common humanity.
We are the same before God, and if this does not increasingly
translate into an ever-deepening self-understanding that we
are the same before one another, we are fooling ourselves.
I heard my friend, Jason Upton, once put it this way, "The
mystery of heaven is we are all God's favorite."

And what of all our highly developed talents and skills and
wealth and grace gifts? Do they not matter? Of course they
do—but only to the extent they become the means by which
we can bless and affirm the sacred worth of other people.
Becoming a real Christian means bringing everything that
once distinguished us and divided us from other people under
the cross of Jesus where it can all be transformed into the
creativity of holy love—the means by which we can uniquely
give ourselves for the sake of other people for the glory of God.

The Prayer

Our Father in heaven, thank you for the cross of Jesus by
which we are crucified to the world and the world to us. Give

me the grace to know who I most truly am, stripped of all the ways by which I have tried to distinguish myself from everyone else. Restore my identity to my simple standing before you, baptized, Spirit-filled, anointed, humble. I pray in Jesus' name, amen.

The Questions

• Does any of today's material rock your world or at least move your understanding to a new place? What is it in us that wants to be better than others? More accomplished? How can we take steps in becoming crucified to the world? What would it look like to distinguish ourselves and our accomplishments for the sake of blessing other people? Can you visualize yourself back in that hospital nursery? How can you get back to living out of that place of inestimable worth and possibility? Can you visualize your baptism? Might the Holy Spirit be revealing deeper meaning from that moment that can break you free from what holds you back?

The Respectability of Conventional Religion

16

1 CORINTHIANS 4:8–13 | Already you have all you want! Already you have become rich! You have begun to reign—and that without us! How I wish that you really had begun to reign

so that we also might reign with you! For it seems to me that God has put us apostles on display at the end of the procession, like those condemned to die in the arena. We have been made a spectacle to the whole universe, to angels as well as to human beings. We are fools for Christ, but you are so wise in Christ! We are weak, but you are strong! You are honored, we are dishonored! To this very hour we go hungry and thirsty, we are in rags, we are brutally treated, we are homeless. We work hard with our own hands. When we are cursed, we bless; when we are persecuted, we endure it; when we are slandered, we answer kindly. We have become the scum of the earth, the garbage of the world—right up to this moment.

Consider This

To those sanctified in Christ Jesus and called to be his holy people (i.e., us):

Some preachers are immediately forgettable while others make a lasting impression. The difference rarely comes down to their delivery. It's all about the message. Still, you don't tend to remember the preacher, but the message, and that's probably as it should be. I am destined to remember a particular sermon I heard in my first year of seminary by a preacher whose name I cannot recall as I heard him only once. And of the sermon, I only remember one sentence. You ready for it? It's a stinger. "Most of you here today are quite content to pursue the American dream for the rest of your lives with a little Jesus overlay."

That's the problem with these Corinthian Christians. They are pursuing the same Corinthian dream and lifestyle mindset as everyone else around them, except theirs has a little Jesus overlay. They want to continue pursuing the respectability of the conventional religion of Corinth with some Christian sauce on it. Said more bluntly, they are all for Jesus, they just aren't too interested in the foolishness of the cross. They wanted to be wise and wealthy and honored by the people around them.

We are fools for Christ, but you are so wise in Christ! We are weak, but you are strong! You are honored, we are dishonored!

Paul offered them the kingdom, but they wanted the world. Actually, they wanted both. Therein lies the big problem. We think we can have both—the kingdom of the world and the kingdom of God. Few of us would brazenly choose the world over Jesus. But there are too few of us who will boldly choose Jesus over the world. And it's not that we don't believe in Jesus and want to walk in the way of the cross. The problem is we simply don't make a choice. We slowly settle into a mushy middle that winds up quite resonant with the lifestyle and values of the culture around us with a little Jesus overlay. There's a technical term for this. It's called "double-mindedness." We are neither hot nor cold, but lukewarm at best.

Paul launches into something of a tirade against these Corinthians. He's a bit angry. I get the sense Paul felt like he had wasted his time with them. The big tragedy is the way the Corinthians were equating this apparent prosperity with the realized rewards of God's kingdom. After all, didn't Jesus come so we could have abundant life?

That's the issue, I think. We readily overlay our cultural understanding of abundance onto the Christian life, when the kingdom idea of abundance means something completely different. Paul touches on it when he says things like:

When we are cursed, we bless; when we are persecuted, we endure it; when we are slandered, we answer kindly.

Abundance is not the wealth of things. Nor is abundance the absence of hardship, suffering, tragedy, or loss. Abundance is the unwavering, powerful presence of God in the midst of hardship, suffering, tragedy, and loss.

So who is ready to step over the line from the respectability of conventional religion into the foolishness of the cross? Who is ready to make the gospel the very substance of their lives, perhaps with a little American overlay? Jesus asks us to choose. When he says, "If anyone would come after me, let him deny himself and take up his cross daily and follow me," he's asking for a definitive choice (Luke 9:23). The greatest gift we can give one another is to love each other enough to not let ourselves fail to choose and slip into the mushy middle of respectable religion. Jesus paid too high a price for that, and besides, we don't want to waste our lives.

Now if you will, permit me a brief sidebar on the issue of wealth. Let me try to be clear. Wealth is neither good nor bad. It can be stewarded to do great harm or great good. The problem with wealth for a Christian is it is inherently decep-tive. Wealth requests the same thing of us that God does—our love. Again, it's not a problem for most of us that we would willingly choose wealth over God. Our problem is the way we are willing to tolerate the ambiguity and risk the deception of not choosing.

Jesus didn't say so much about money because he wanted us to increase our tithe to the church, but because he knew we could not serve two masters, that double-mindedness would ultimately mean disaster. From the time of Jesus' ministry on earth to the present day, the issue of idolatry has had less to do with Baal and little statues and everything to do with money. Jesus doesn't care about our money. He cares about our souls. He loves us. It's why wealthy people often need much more intensive discipleship; their wealth brings with it a very challenging calling, and many a soul has been shipwrecked from the fearful fleeing of that calling. I want you to be boldly faithful, generously spirited, gloriously alive disciples of Jesus Christ.

The Prayer

Our Father in heaven, thank you for the cross of Jesus, by which I am crucified to the world and the world to me. I confess, the values of the world and my broken under-standing of abundance distort my faith. Lead me to understand the abundance of "on earth as it is in heaven" and to truly grasp and experience the joy of the Lord. I want to be a real Christian; not settling for a little Jesus overlay onto my otherwise easy and indulgent life. I pray in Jesus' name, amen.

The Questions

- Have you decided to follow Jesus, really? No turning back? What are the effects of respectable, conventional religion on our churches? What kind of witness and impact does it lead those churches to have on the world? What would stepping out of the comfort zone mean for you? What might it cost you? What might it cost you to stay in the comfort of convention?

17 The Two Words That Signify Mature, Adult Christianity

1 CORINTHIANS 4:14–17 | I am writing this not to shame you but to warn you as my dear children. Even if you had ten thousand guardians in Christ, you do not have many fathers, for in Christ Jesus I became your father through the gospel. Therefore I urge you to imitate me. For this reason I have sent to you Timothy, my son whom I love, who is faithful in the Lord. He will remind you of my way of life in Christ Jesus, which agrees with what I teach everywhere in every church.

Consider This

To those sanctified in Christ Jesus and called to be his holy people (i.e., us):

So what are the two words from today's text that signify mature, adult Christianity? No, the two words aren't "thank you," though that would be good. See if you can locate the two words I'm referring to in today's text. They are the two words that every adult Christian must seriously consider adding to their discipleship vocabulary regarding the relationship they have with other believers in their care—and by "adult" I don't mean over the age of eighteen, but rather a mature disciple of Jesus Christ.

And did you note the assumption I just dropped into that last sentence? Yes, one of the marks of adult Christianity is having other people in your care and over whom you watch in love. No, it doesn't necessarily mean you are in a formal one-on-one discipleship training relationship or even in a small group with them—though this is usually a good thing. Adult Christianity implies that I have come to the realization that others are paying attention to "my way of life in Christ Jesus." It doesn't mean that I am in some kind of official position of Christian leader in a church or otherwise Christian organization. It certainly doesn't mean that everyone identifies me as that guy who is always at church every time the doors are opened.

Those two words . . . have you found them yet? Before I spoil the fun, let me back up to a phrase from today's text I noted in the last paragraph. To bring even more explicit clarity to the point, an adult Christian is one who, over time, has an established "way of life in Christ Jesus." It doesn't mean they go about wearing their religion on their sleeve or saying the name of Jesus in every other sentence in casual conversation. To have a "way of life in Christ Jesus" means I have stepped out of the crowd and left the bland respectability of conventional religion behind. It means I have taken the responsibility to seriously ask myself if I have a "way of life in Christ Jesus," and how would I know it if I did. Taking it a step further, adult Christianity means I have given at least one other person a set of keys to my life in some way, shape, or form.

We don't tend to gravitate toward these two words I'm emphasizing today because we would be presumptuous to say them or somehow prideful or haughty. When it comes to stepping up to the plate of Big League Christianity, most of us shrink back. We are content to stay in Little League. We were all meant to ultimately play in the major leagues. It's just too easy and respectable to cloak ourselves in false humility and play down instead of up. And no, this does not mean becoming a super serious Christian that no one wants to be around. Mature adult Christian faith means just the opposite. It means having a "way of life in Christ Jesus" that is distinctive, surprising, at times quiet and at other times bold, and in the final analysis—irresistible.

So these two words—when we say them we are effectively writing a check to someone else or to multiple someones. And in light of that metaphor there are really only two reasons we refuse to say them. We either (1) know we don't have the money in the bank, or (2) we aren't willing to invest it. And let's be clear about number 1. The money in the bank I'm referring to is not some savings account you have created. It's a checking account funded by none other than the Holy Spirit. The money is there. You have to spend it to know.

So let's get to it. What are the two words from today's text that signify mature, adult Christianity? Just in case you haven't figured them out yet, I am going to end with them. *Imitate me.*

The Prayer

Our Father in heaven, thank you for your Son and our Lord, Jesus Christ. Thank you for the Holy Spirit, who empowers us to follow Jesus and imitate his way of life. Wake me up to the fact that others are imitating me—for better or for worse. Let my life become not a religious performance but a holy act of love; an irresistible freedom—even a contagious, uncontainable joy. Forgive me for my lazy Little League mentality. In Jesus' name, amen.

The Questions

- How would you articulate to yourself your "way of life in Christ Jesus"? What did that look like yesterday? Be specific. What will it mean, in particular, for you to have a "way of life in Christ Jesus" today? Even if only one thing. What keeps you from being willing to invite others to imitate you? Are you ready to write that check? Will you write it anyway?

18 | The Problem with Saying "Lord Willing and the Creek Don't Rise"

1 CORINTHIANS 4:18–21 ESV | Some are arrogant, as though I were not coming to you. But I will come to you soon, if the Lord wills, and I will find out not the talk of these arrogant people but their power. For the kingdom of God does not consist in talk but in power. What do you wish? Shall I come to you with a rod, or with love in a spirit of gentleness?

Consider This

To those sanctified in Christ Jesus and called to be his holy people (i.e., us):

There are at least two directions we could take with today's text. On the one hand, we could go down the "I'm going to open up a can on you Corinthians" track. We could get into the tricky issues of church discipline and where it may be warranted and how utterly foreign this idea is to a twenty-first-century American Christian. We could talk about strategies of confronting rebellion and dissension built on rogue and even arrogant authority. There's a good conversation to be had about the difference between leading with firm authority and authoritarianism. I'm going to leave those for another day.

Instead, I want to address what I may have actually flown past in prior years and paid no attention to. In other words, it was a throwaway phrase for me. And, in fact, it's actually that kind of phrase for many people. It has become a bit of a cliché. I don't think that was the case for Paul. Our words matter very much. Even though Paul says the kingdom of God is not a matter of talk, still our words matter. This little phrase in today's text points to a deep dispositional reality in the apostle. It shows the attitude and mentality of a person who lives under authority.

But I will come to you soon, if the Lord wills, and I will find out not the talk of these arrogant people but their power.

Did you see it? "If the Lord wills." Paul conditioned any and every significant and perhaps not so significant decision in his life on those four words: "If the Lord wills." You've heard it and like me, probably said it. "We plan to be there," we might say, and then add on a quick, "Lord willing and the creek don't rise." It's another way of saying, "I am dead serious about keeping my word on this, short of a hurricane or earthquake." In other words, "I'm doggedly committed to this unless the devil stops me."

Despite the fact that many people use this phrase with real sincerity, we have reduced it to an idiom. For Paul, I am convinced this was no idiom. It was his "way of life in Christ Jesus." He lived in constant, humble, joyful submission to the ever-unfolding will of God. James makes the same point in his letter when he says,

> Now listen, you who say, "Today or tomorrow we will go to this or that city, spend a year there, carry on business and make money." Why, you do not even know

what will happen tomorrow. What is your life? You are a mist that appears for a little while and then vanishes. Instead, you ought to say, "If it is the Lord's will, we will live and do this or that." (4:13–15)

At the end of the day this comes down to the issue of sovereignty. Who is sovereign in our lives? Is it me and my plans or is it the will and the willingness of God? It's a real journey to get to the place where we truly come to this way of life. It's not as simple as saying it, though at times this can be a helpful reminder. (The problem is the way it can be an outright untruth.) This conviction, far from a colloquial or even sentimental saying, reflects an unwavering trust in God. That's where we want to be—possessing unwavering, humble trust in God.

The Prayer

Our Father in heaven, indeed this is where I want to be—an unwavering, humble trust in you. I want to live so filled with your Spirit and governed by your mind that I think thoughts after yours and that my plans begin to naturally reflect your will. Teach me to think, live, and even say, "If the Lord is willing," submitting my every agenda to yours in both large matters and small things. Let my submission become bold and my humility palpable—for your glory. I pray in Jesus' name, amen.

The Questions

• How tightly do you cling to your own plans? Are you convinced that your plans are going to be better for you than God's plans? What is your greatest fear about submitting to the will of God and God's plans in advance of knowing anything about those plans? Does your prayer life include the regularity of inquiring of the Lord concerning your plans or are you more inclined to simply ask God to bless your plans?

Why Sexual Immorality Is Not the Problem 19

1 CORINTHIANS 5:1–13 | It is actually reported that there is sexual immorality among you, and of a kind that even pagans do not tolerate: A man is sleeping with his father's wife. And you are proud! Shouldn't you rather have gone into mourning and have put out of your fellowship the man who has been doing this? For my part, even though I am not physically present, I am with you in spirit. As one who is present with you in this way, I have already passed judgment in the name of our Lord Jesus on the one who has been doing this. So when you are assembled and I am with you in spirit, and the power of our Lord Jesus is present, hand this man over to Satan for the destruction of the flesh, so that his spirit may be saved on the day of the Lord.

Your boasting is not good. Don't you know that a little yeast leavens the whole batch of dough? Get rid of the old yeast, so that you may be a new unleavened batch—as you really are.

For Christ, our Passover lamb, has been sacrificed. Therefore let us keep the Festival, not with the old bread leavened with malice and wickedness, but with the unleavened bread of sincerity and truth.

I wrote to you in my letter not to associate with sexually immoral people—not at all meaning the people of this world who are immoral, or the greedy and swindlers, or idolaters. In that case you would have to leave this world. But now I am writing to you that you must not associate with anyone who claims to be a brother or sister but is sexually immoral or greedy, an idolater or slanderer, a drunkard or swindler. Do not even eat with such people.

What business is it of mine to judge those outside the church? Are you not to judge those inside? God will judge those outside. "Expel the wicked person from among you."

Consider This

To those sanctified in Christ Jesus and called to be his holy people (i.e., us):

Today we have a challenge. The text is longer than usual and much more complex and nuanced in its arguments. Even more difficult, it deals with church discipline, a concept utterly foreign to us; at least those of us in the United States of America. The final difficulty lies in its subject matter: immorality and, notably, sexual immorality, which is a hotly debated issue not only in the culture around us but in some of our churches. Given these realities, it would be impossible for me to give adequate treatment to a text like this in this venue and format. Additionally, it would be ill-advised to speak beyond generalities in my attempt. I can neither back away from the text, nor can I fully dive in. So what am I to do? I will simply make some broad propositional observations:

1. We are going to hear a lot from Paul on the subject of sexual immorality in this letter. It's not because sexual sin lives in another category from other sins. The reason Paul engages it head-on is because it was a particularly pervasive category of sin in Corinth.

2. Because the boundaries of sexual behavior were almost non-existent in ancient Corinth, people who had become followers of Jesus would have brought these kinds of patterns right into the church.

3. The big problem with the Corinthians is they wanted to reclassify certain categories of sin—namely the sins they were accustomed to—as "not sin." Paul said the effect of this would be to do great damage to the whole community.

Don't you know that a little yeast leavens the whole batch of dough? Get rid of the old yeast, so that you may be a new unleavened batch—as you really are.

Paul shows his cards early on that he will be evenhanded when it comes to sexual sin, not singling out one sin over another. He will name most of them before it is all said and done here. It is also interesting to note how he lists sexual immorality as part of a larger and much broader list of sins in this context.

4. Paul is urging the young church to come to grips with the powerful "as you really are" new reality the Holy Spirit was bringing about through the gospel of Jesus Christ. This new reality? Deliverance from the power of sin.

5. The particular issue at hand in today's text is that of the church tolerating and even condoning sexual immorality. Yes, Paul is concerned for the salvation of this guy who was sleeping with his stepmother, but his greater concern is for the life of the church. (Can you imagine the letter that Paul might write to the Roman Catholic Church concerning the sexual abuse scandals among the priesthood?!)

6. So, throw the guy out? It sounds harsh, but remember Paul's chief aim in Corinth is to participate with the Holy Spirit's work to make Jesus known in the world through the distinctive presence of a community of people who are so compellingly and winsomely and beautifully different that the sin sick, broken people of the world will be irresistibly drawn into their fellowship.

7. Consider Paul's options. (A) Look the other way, and let it go. There are, after all, other problems to deal with. (B) Ask the man to cease his association with the church as an assembly until such time as he had ended this relationship. (C) Create a restoration process whereby the man is graciously yet firmly confronted, put on leave from the public gathering of the church, and given a pathway toward recovery and reincorpo-ration into the church.

The problem with A: not only is the inevitable ruin of the man at issue here but the corruption of the church. A posture of tolerating sin inevitably leads toward its outright affirmation later. The problem with B: it seems harsh and a far cry from redemptive. It looks and feels like shaming and shunning, which seem like the last thing Jesus would ever do. It's why I think Paul chose C.

Why do I think this? To borrow an old legal term, here's my theory of the case. Paul forbade the people of the church to associate with unrepentant sinners who claimed to be brothers or sisters in Christ. Paul did not forbid the community to have contact with sexually immoral people in Corinth who were not part of the church. How could they ever witness to such people if they couldn't engage with them? On the other hand, what kind of distinctive witness would they have if the people in their church were no different than the people outside of it? In fact, in this case, what this guy was up to with his stepmother was even forbidden by the sex-crazed Corinthians, creating the ironic situation whereby the church was affirming behavior not even allowed by the world around them. I think Paul was actually creating a context whereby the people of the church could relate to this man in redemptive and hopefully restorative ways. Follow the logic?

Bottom line: having sex with your stepmother is a problem, but it is not *the* problem. The problem for Paul is a church without integrity. The problem is the refusal of God's people to call sin "sin" and deal with it redemptively.

The big issue here, as noted, is not sexual immorality, but calling sin "not sin." In our present context, none of us would likely contend for the virtue or even permissibility of the son having sexual relations with his stepmother. In other words, we would not want to call sin "not sin" in this instance. While there is no reference in this text to other particular dimensions of sexual brokenness, it strikes me that this is precisely what is happening in our culture—many people within the church are contending that what has long been considered sexual sin should now be called "not sin."

Again, sexual immorality is not *the* problem. The issue is the growing willingness of the church to call sin "not sin." Once this happens, the church ceases to be a pathway toward redemption for people whose broken sexuality has broken their lives. In other words, if you are part of a church and you have been broken by a sin the church no longer considers a sin, then the church can't help you.

The Prayer

Our Father in heaven, hallowed be your name. And hallowed be your church. Forgive us for the ways we have singled out sins and shamed sinners. Teach us what it looks like to forgive sin and embrace the sinner. Save us from the perilous pathway of calling sin "not sin." Give us the courage to not so much take a stand against sin but stand on the premises and promises of your Word in the power of your Spirit. Teach us to kneel down as sinners with sinners, allowing you to be the judge in your way and your time. Lead us through the challenging times we face, knowing that the way we walk will determine our destination. In Jesus' name, amen.

The Questions

- Given this line of thinking, with which you may not agree, how might Paul respond to the issue of homosexuality in today's world? What does it look like to embrace a person without affirming their sin? How does discipline play into that reality? What is the long-term impact of calling or redefining sin as "not sin"? Where does that lead?

The Church at Corinth as a Bad *Jerry Springer* Rerun

20

1 CORINTHIANS 6:1–11 | If any of you has a dispute with another, do you dare to take it before the ungodly for judgment instead of before the Lord's people? Or do you not know that the Lord's people will judge the world? And if you are to judge the world, are you not competent to judge trivial cases? Do you not know that we will judge angels? How much more the things of this life! Therefore, if you have disputes about such matters, do you ask for a ruling from those whose way of life is scorned in the church? I say this to shame you. Is it possible that there is nobody among you wise enough to judge a dispute between believers? But instead, one brother takes another to court—and this in front of unbelievers!

The very fact that you have lawsuits among you means you have been completely defeated already. Why not rather be wronged? Why not rather be cheated? Instead, you yourselves cheat and do wrong, and you do this to your brothers and sisters. Or do you not know that wrongdoers will not inherit the kingdom of God? Do not be deceived: Neither the sexually immoral nor idolaters nor adulterers nor men who have sex with men nor thieves nor the greedy nor drunkards nor slanderers nor swindlers will inherit the kingdom of God. And that is what some of you were. But you were washed, you were sanctified, you were justified in the name of the Lord Jesus Christ and by the Spirit of our God.

Consider This

To those sanctified in Christ Jesus and called to be his holy people (i.e., us):

For all the things the Christian faith has been made out to be and all the ways it has been framed and conformed to fit into this project or that program, perhaps its most fundamental premise has been mostly missed. Paul will not let it go. A good summary of it comes in the last verse of today's text.

But you were washed, you were sanctified, you were justified in the name of the Lord Jesus Christ and by the Spirit of our God.

Here's what Paul did not mean by this: your fundamental problem of eternal separation from God because of sin has been solved so that when you die you will go to heaven. Now you can get on with your life and while you are at it, spread the word that other people can have their fundamental problem of eternal separation from God because of sin solved so they will go to heaven when they die.

So, is it true that every last one of us has a fundamental problem of eternal separation from God because of sin that must be solved so that when we die we will not perish but have eternal life? Yes. It's true. So what's my point?

For Paul, salvation by grace through faith is not primarily a present transaction that will impact a future outcome. For Paul, salvation by grace through faith is a future outcome that has become a present reality. Salvation and the entry into eternal life is not something that happens when we die. Salvation and the entry into eternal life is what happens now, when we personally own that our fundamental problem is eternal separation from God. Salvation begins when we surrender the sovereignty of our self-rule to the sovereignty of God. Salvation continues as we walk the daily journey of living into the new reality brought about by the life, death, resurrection, and ascension of Jesus Christ and the coming of the Holy Spirit—all of which is signed and signaled by the ultimate truth of heaven and earth: Jesus Christ is Lord.

The common thread running through all of the apostle's teaching is as follows: the resurrection of Jesus Christ from the dead and the coming of the Holy Spirit means the coming age has already begun. Salvation by grace through faith means you now live in the realm of the kingdom of God in the age of the Holy Spirit. What was impossible for you before is now possible. The power of the Holy Spirit is now available to deliver you from any and all sins and give you unprecedented, unending life. Yes, the kingdom will come in all its glory at the end of this present evil age, but the *big news* is it has now begun. As a result of this, stop wasting your life and my time. No more divisions over stupid stuff. Be done with sexual sin. Stop bringing lawsuits against one another in the courts of Babylon. You are the church. Stop parading your messed-up lives before the world like a *Jerry Springer* rerun. You are the living, breathing temple of the presence of God on earth. He is here within and among you. Your calling is to simply reflect and share this reality with the world around you.

Too often we approach the Christian faith as a coping strategy to get through life, or as a self-improvement strategy to enhance our already good lives, or a life insurance policy to extend life beyond the grave, or a fire insurance policy to keep life out of eternal death. All the while, the Christian faith is *life* itself—*life at a completely different level—life at the level of eternal quality; because it is the very life of God lived at the human level—right here, right now*. It is *life* that shines in the darkness of the deepest pits of human despair. It is *life* at the moment of death and the moment after that. This is where Paul is coming from. This is his point. This is the underlying and overarching assumption beneath and above everything he says and writes and does. When he says to "imitate me," and to follow his "way of life in Christ Jesus," this is what he means. This is not a behavioral-management program he's running. It's an *eternal life* reality he's proclaiming. I better stop now.

The Prayer

Our Father in heaven, hallowed be your name. Your kingdom come. Your will be done; on earth as it is in heaven.

Wake me up to the depths of this prayer. Open my eyes of my heart to perceive the immensity of eternal life—right here and right now. Help me grasp how I have misunderstood and misappropriated the life of Christ in me. I don't want to waste another day. Come, Holy Spirit, and make this life count for all God intends. In Jesus' name, amen.

The Questions

- So how have you primarily understood the Christian faith and life? Fire insurance? Life insurance? Coping strategy? Self-improvement? Legalistic nightmare? Or the *present experience of the age to come which is eternal life*? How has that changed over the years? Is eternal life something you are hoping for or that you have faith will one day happen or is it actually happening now in your present experience? How would you describe it? If you are not sure of this reality would you be willing to ask God to reveal it to you by the power of the Word and Holy Spirit?

Why We Need Track Shoes When It Comes to Sexuality Immorality   21

1 CORINTHIANS 6:12–20 | "I have the right to do anything," you say—but not everything is beneficial. "I have the right to do anything"—but I will not be mastered by anything. You say,

"Food for the stomach and the stomach for food, and God will destroy them both." The body, however, is not meant for sexual immorality but for the Lord, and the Lord for the body. By his power God raised the Lord from the dead, and he will raise us also. Do you not know that your bodies are members of Christ himself? Shall I then take the members of Christ and unite them with a prostitute? Never! Do you not know that he who unites himself with a prostitute is one with her in body? For it is said, "The two will become one flesh." But whoever is united with the Lord is one with him in spirit.

Flee from sexual immorality. All other sins a person commits are outside the body, but whoever sins sexually, sins against their own body. Do you not know that your bodies are temples of the Holy Spirit, who is in you, whom you have received from God? You are not your own; you were bought at a price. Therefore honor God with your bodies.

Consider This

To those sanctified in Christ Jesus and called to be his holy people (i.e., us):

POP QUIZ: What do the first-century Corinthians have in common with twenty-first-century Americans?

Hint: The first seven words of today's text.

"I have the right to do anything"

Yes, these seven little words could be our biggest problem. In Corinth, this was the mentality of a so-called "spiritual" person, someone whose life had been illuminated by the superior religion of the wisdom of the age. Again, they wanted to bring it right into the church. It was especially handy when it came to their penchant for prostitutes.

Come to think of it, it sounds a little reminiscent of the ethos behind the sexual revolution in this country. It goes something like this: "What two consenting adults do in the privacy of their own home is their own business and they have every right to do it. What business is it of the government to tell people who they can marry and who they can't and so forth?"

And what business is it of the church to dole out rights? Answer: the church does not do business in the realm of rights. That is not our language or framework. The real issue is not our rights, but righteousness in our relationships; by righteousness I mean the inside-out expression of the holy love of God and neighbor.

These Corinthians reasoned that their bodies were temporal and would ultimately be done away with, so what's the big deal with a little philandering? After all, *"Food for the stomach and the stomach for food,"* right? Eat, drink, and be merry! "Come on," they would say, "We have the right to do anything we want to do." They believed in the immortality of the soul. Christians believe in the resurrection of the body. Because the resurrection of the body is a core doctrine of the Christian faith, we take a very high view of the human body. The human body is sacred and must be cherished and guarded against corruption.

The body, however, is not meant for sexual immorality but for the Lord, and the Lord for the body. By his power God raised the Lord from the dead, and he will raise us also.

Do you see how Paul so artfully confronts the false teaching of the Corinthians with the sound doctrine of the gospel of Jesus Christ? People are going to do what people are going to do, but there is no need for the church to be unclear about what it believes, and there is certainly no need to change its course to conform to the cultural tides of the age. The church need not be mean-spirited or cavalier or caustic—just clear.

Scripture offers an equal-opportunity rebuke to any and all forms of sexual immorality. People want to know why the church tends to put so much emphasis on this. It's because the Bible puts so much emphasis on it. As noted earlier, sexual sin is not in a separate category from other sin, however, it does receive a lot of careful attention from Scripture. Somewhere along the way, the church unfortunately equated sexual immorality with sex in general, and we still haven't recovered. Scripture quite robustly affirms sexual union in the context of marriage, but outside of marriage it is destructive.

Flee from sexual immorality. All other sins a person commits are outside the body, but whoever sins sexually, sins against their own body. Do you not know that your bodies are temples of the Holy Spirit, who is in you, whom you have received from God? You are not your own; you were bought at a price. Therefore honor God with your bodies.

There's something about sexual immorality that cuts to the very heart of our relationship with God. We want to think of our relationship with God as primarily a spiritual reality. That's how the Corinthians were letting themselves off the hook. According to Scripture, our relationship with

God seems to primarily be a bodily thing. Our "spirits" or our "inner person" are not the temple of the Holy Spirit. Our physical human bodies are temples of the Holy Spirit.

Let's close with the two admonitions from today's text:

Flee from sexual immorality. . . . Therefore honor God with your bodies.

We don't flee sexual immorality because sex is a bad thing. It's because sex is a good thing. In fact, it may just be one of the greatest ways two married people can honor God with their bodies. Sex is not a right for anyone. It is a sacred privilege of those called to be married. More on that to come.

The Prayer

Our Father in heaven, hallowed be your name. Your kingdom come. Your will be done, on earth as it is in heaven. Thank you for calling us to be holy as you are holy. Thank you for the arresting and compelling vision of holiness we see in your Son, Jesus. Forgive us for messing up that word so badly. Thank you that my physical body is a temple of the Holy Spirit. Awaken me to all the implications of this reality. I want to experience it to the full. I am living beneath this now. Come, Holy Spirit, and from my sexuality to my weight and fitness, lead me to bodily holiness in a beautiful way. I pray in Jesus' name, amen.

The Questions

- Why do you think sexual immorality is seemingly singled out in a category of its own in Scripture? What are the implications of that? What would it look like for you to "flee from sexual immorality"? What images does the word "flee" conjure up in your mind? How can that be strategized and actualized in your life? What would it mean for you to take steps to "honor God with your body"?

22 What a True Sexual Revolution Might Look Like

1 CORINTHIANS 7:1–9 | Now for the matters you wrote about: "It is good for a man not to have sexual relations with a woman." But since sexual immorality is occurring, each man should have sexual relations with his own wife, and each woman with her own husband. The husband should fulfill his marital duty to his wife, and likewise the wife to her husband. The wife does not have authority over her own body but yields it to her husband. In the same way, the husband does not have authority over his own body but yields it to his wife. Do not deprive each other except perhaps by mutual consent and for a time, so that you may devote yourselves to prayer. Then come together again so that Satan will not tempt you because of your lack of self-control. I say this as a concession, not as a command. I wish that all of you were as I am. But each of you has your own gift from God; one has this gift, another has that.

Now to the unmarried and the widows I say: It is good for them to stay unmarried, as I do. But if they cannot control themselves, they should marry, for it is better to marry than to burn with passion.

Consider This

To those sanctified in Christ Jesus and called to be his holy people (i.e., us):

Next to the "slaves obey your masters" verse, today's text may have some of the most misinterpreted, misapplied, and abusive appropriations in the whole of Scripture. Here are a few of the more egregious errors:

1. Sex is bad.

2. Marriage is only a concession and necessity for those who cannot control their lustful passions.

3. Singleness is a gift.

4. Marriage is a distraction from the ministry of the gospel.

5. Celibacy is superior to marriage.

6. Women have a duty to cater to, fulfill, and even obey the sexual desires of their husbands.

And we will stop there. The Corinthians had a really distorted view of human sexuality. This is what happens when our understanding of sexuality comes primarily from biological and sociological frameworks. When we begin there, we inevitably develop our theological understandings to support our biological and sociological frameworks. Paul will not have it. He begins his teaching on human sexuality with a biblical and theological framework. This leads Paul to a completely different set of holdings than he is often saddled with by ancient and modern interpreters alike.

Following are what I consider to be the biblical and theological correctives to the list above.

1. Sex is a good gift from God wherein the unity, diversity, and complementary nature of human beings is celebrated.

2. Monogamous marriage between a man and a woman is not a concession to sexual desire but a gift of the Holy Spirit.

3. Celibacy, not singleness, is a gift of the Holy Spirit. There's a difference.

4. Rather than a distraction from the gospel, marriage creates a vocational dimension of advancing the ministry of the gospel.

5. Neither celibacy nor marriage is to be elevated over the other.

6. Marriage is not a hierarchical, power-oriented relationship. Paul takes great care here to define marriage as a mutually submissive and mutually beneficial relationship. Each belongs to the other. One cannot claim a debt on the other, yet each can assert their indebtedness to the other. In marriage, it's always, "I owe you," and never "You owe me."

The big takeaways for me: begin with divine revelation not human anthropology—with theology not sociology. The biblical vision must shape the human condition and not the other way around. Theological wisdom must set the framework in which to understand and interpret human experience and not the other way around. Many of the problems we face in the twenty-first-century church can largely be attributed to getting this precisely backward.

The Prayer

Our Father in heaven, hallowed be your name. Your kingdom come. Your will be done, on earth as it is in heaven. Thank you for speaking so clearly and practically on these everyday matters of our lives. Forgive us for exalting our human-centered and earth-bound experience and disciplines over the divine revelation of your Word. Forgive us for exalting the accumulation of knowledge over the pursuit of wisdom. Train us to humble ourselves before you that we might be taught the ways of grace and truth, of love and wisdom—in all things. We pray in Jesus' name, amen.

The Questions

- In the old days, happiness and holiness were practically synonymous. Now they are largely two different things. How would you differentiate between the terms and how might your life bring them together again? How are you most challenged by today's text and reflection? How do you relate to the biblical concept of mutuality in marriage as always, "I owe you," and never "You owe me"?

23 | Why We Need Sound, Orthodox Biblical Scholars

1 CORINTHIANS 7:10–16 | To the married I give this command (not I, but the Lord): A wife must not separate from her husband. But if she does, she must remain unmarried or else be reconciled to her husband. And a husband must not divorce his wife.

To the rest I say this (I, not the Lord): If any brother has a wife who is not a believer and she is willing to live with him, he must not divorce her. And if a woman has a husband who is not a believer and he is willing to live with her, she must not divorce him. For the unbelieving husband has been sanctified through his wife, and the unbelieving wife has been sanctified through her believing husband. Otherwise your children would be unclean, but as it is, they are holy.

But if the unbeliever leaves, let it be so. The brother or the sister is not bound in such circumstances; God has called us to live in peace. How do you know, wife, whether you will save your husband? Or, how do you know, husband, whether you will save your wife?

Consider This

To those sanctified in Christ Jesus and called to be his holy people (i.e., us):

The Bible is an exceedingly complex book. One of the great gifts of the Protestant Reformation was that the Bible was made accessible to people outside of the priesthood. In many ways, the Bible can be understood by anyone. This is referred to as the "perspicuity," or transparent, reading of the text. In other words, it means what it plainly says, and a person doesn't need a graduate degree to understand it. In another sense, we are dealing with an ancient text written over the course of fifteen hundred years, on three continents, in three different languages (none of which are still spoken), by more than forty different authors. And did I mention the one book we call the Bible is actually sixty-six different individual books/ letters in and of themselves? Through the centuries, biblical scholars—women and men who have given their lives to the study of this book—have given us inestimable gifts of insight and understanding through their faithful interpretation.

I write the Daily Text with a deep sense of responsibility both to God and to you, my readers. I write it prayerfully, and yet I do not write it alone. I stand on the shoulders of two thousand years' worth of biblical study and interpretation. I stand on the shoulders of scholars who have worked tirelessly to "rightly divide the word of truth"; one generation faithfully handing the baton to the next. Dr. Gordon Fee, a renowned Bible scholar from the Pentecostal tradition, teaches me daily from his work on 1 Corinthians. In seminary, I sat under the biblical instruction of Dr. Ben Witherington III whose teaching on 1 Corinthians continues to shape my approach and understanding of the text.

To be clear, some biblical scholars have done inestimable damage to the church's interpretation and understanding of Scripture. We need not let their misguided (albeit often well-intentioned) work taint our trust in the whole enterprise of biblical interpretation. The answer to bad teaching is not no teaching. It is good teaching.

This is a difficult passage and subject to rife misinterpretations. I want to point out something very important and easily missed in this seventh chapter of the letter: the context. It's important to recognize Paul is not setting out to write canon law on marriage and divorce for the church. We must remember what 1 Corinthians is—an ancient letter. As well, we must remember it is actually part of a larger trail of correspondence between Paul and this church. We have two of what may be as many as four or more letters in that exchange. This letter is a direct and somewhat detailed response to the letter sent to Paul by the church, which was ostensibly a response to Paul's earlier letter to them.

Now, the contextual feature that often gets completely ignored in the interpretation of 1 Corinthians 7 is the opening line.

Now for the matters you wrote about: "It is good for a man not to have sexual relations with a woman."

In all that follows, Paul is responding to this statement from their letter to him. He delves into tangential matters and, at times, claims authority and, at other times, simply asserts his own opinion. The bottom line is that Paul is dealing with a situation in which it seems women wanted to dissolve their marriages because of their highly spiritualized understanding of life derived from the ever-present "wisdom" teachings in Corinth. They have been called the "eschatological women" because they believed they had already realized the "resurrection of the dead" in a spiritualized form and that they existed spiritually in the realm of angelic beings with all sorts of spiritual powers. In this spiritualized state, the body was of no use and marriage and sex and the like were distractions from the former age that for them had passed away. And just because Paul is addressing a very particular issue in first-century Corinth does not mean it has no application for us today. The point is that the context conditions the application for us, sometimes in massive ways and other times in nuanced distinctions.

If we can't understand what Paul's letter meant to the Corinthians in the first century, we have little hope of properly understanding it in the twenty-first century, and, in fact, we are in grave danger of bringing in our own extra-biblical understandings of divorce and remarriage, and thereby making the text mean something it never intended to mean. For instance, texts like today's have been egregiously misappropriated in ways that shame women into remaining in abusive marriages.

Are you seeing the complexity of this? This is why we need sound, faithful biblical scholars in the church. If you know one, call them today and thank them for the exceedingly challenging, hidden, and too often thankless labor of their life. It matters greatly.

The Prayer

Our Father in heaven, hallowed be your name. Your kingdom come. Your will be done on earth as it is in heaven. Thank you for your Word and for the countless men and women who have given their lives to transmit it across the ages, to translate it for every nation, tribe, and tongue, to exegete and interpret it with deep devotion and exquisite care. Convict us all to take Scripture more seriously. Our life depends on it. In Jesus' name, amen.

The Questions

• Do you tend to trust or suspect the work of biblical scholars? Why? Are you growing in the conviction that the better and more careful we are able to read Scripture the better disciples we will become?

24 Why Be a Coach When You Are Called to Be a Player?

1 CORINTHIANS 7:17–31 | Nevertheless, each person should live as a believer in whatever situation the Lord has assigned to them, just as God has called them. This is the rule I lay down in all the churches. Was a man already circumcised when he was called? He should not become uncircumcised.

Was a man uncircumcised when he was called? He should not be circumcised. Circumcision is nothing and uncircumcision is nothing. Keeping God's commands is what counts. Each person should remain in the situation they were in when God called them.

Were you a slave when you were called? Don't let it trouble you—although if you can gain your freedom, do so. For the one who was a slave when called to faith in the Lord is the Lord's freed person; similarly, the one who was free when called is Christ's slave. You were bought at a price; do not become slaves of human beings. Brothers and sisters, each person, as responsible to God, should remain in the situation they were in when God called them.

Now about virgins: I have no command from the Lord, but I give a judgment as one who by the Lord's mercy is trustworthy. Because of the present crisis, I think that it is good for a man to remain as he is. Are you pledged to a woman? Do not seek to be released. Are you free from such a commitment? Do not look for a wife. But if you do marry, you have not sinned; and if a virgin marries, she has not sinned. But those who marry will face many troubles in this life, and I want to spare you this.

What I mean, brothers and sisters, is that the time is short. From now on those who have wives should live as if they do not; those who mourn, as if they did not; those who are happy, as if they were not; those who buy something, as if it were not theirs to keep; those who use the things of the world, as if not engrossed in them. For this world in its present form is passing away.

Consider This

To those sanctified in Christ Jesus and called to be his holy people (i.e., us):

If I've seen it happen once, I've seen it a hundred times. I've seen it happen with two different kinds of people. Here's the scenario. On the one hand, a person has a dramatic conversion, leaves behind their former way of life, and begins to diligently reorient their life around the lordship of Jesus Christ. It's an awesome sight to behold. In the other instance, a person has been in the church for years faithfully going through the motions but with little sense of a dynamic experience of relationship with God. Something happens in this person's life, a crisis or an awakening, and all the lights come on, the dots connect, and they come alive to the Holy Spirit and it all finally makes sense. They become passionate about following Jesus and are ready to do whatever he says, whenever, wherever, and however. This, too, is a glorious sight to behold.

So far so good, until they start realizing they have become something of an outlier, both in their everyday world and even in their local church. Many soon lose interest in their former line of work and begin to think perhaps they are called to quit their job, go to seminary, pursue ordination, and enter full-time ministry. Maybe they are, but in most cases—having seen this enacted hundreds of times now—I would say probably not.

Nevertheless, each person should live as a believer in whatever situation the Lord has assigned to them, just as God has called them. This is the rule I lay down in all the churches.

The situation Paul was dealing with in Corinth was not exactly analogous, but we can glean some clear guidance for the situation I outlined. In Paul's situation, people felt they had to leave their former station (Gentile/Jew, married/unmarried, slave/free) in order to fulfill their new calling. In other words, in order to live out their new way of life they needed to change their status, relationships, social station, and so forth—because of the dramatic change in their life, they needed a decisive change in their social arrangement. Paul said absolutely not.

Are you seeing the analogy? The challenge in today's church scenarios is we have basically two options: become a clergy person or otherwise get hired by the church or another ministry *or* just be a layperson. This is a big problem. This notion that a person is just a layperson is nothing short of tragic. It's another way of saying, "I can only go to the game in my present state, but I could never really play on the field. Okay, sure I could work in the concessions stands or be an usher or any number of other volunteer roles, but I can't really be a player in this game unless I quit my job, go to seminary, get ordained, and so forth."

Imagine going to a college football game (or pick your sport) this Saturday, arriving at your seat in the bleachers, and seeing the incredulous sight of the two opposing teams made up entirely of coaches. What kind of disastrous game would that be? In the aggregate, that's exactly the kind of scene we are seeing played out in large parts of the church. The only people allowed to play are the professionals (i.e., the coaches) while all the players have to sit in the stands or, at best, sell hotdogs and cokes to the other players who are sitting in the stands watching the disaster of a game full of coaches doing all the playing.

The church needs coaches for sure and some in the situations I outlined are called to be coaches (and I employ the term loosely rather than technically to make my point). But what the church most needs are thousands upon millions of players—imaginatively playing at most every conceivable vocation in the world.

Each person should remain in the situation they were in when God called them.

In short, unless you have the clear calling to join the coaching staff, don't leave your present station. That's probably the place the Lord needs you the most. It's likely time to double down in your discipleship.

The Prayer

Our Father in heaven, hallowed be your name. Your kingdom come. Your will be done, on earth as it is in heaven. Thank you for the way you call every single baptized follower of Jesus into ministry. Forgive us for the ways we have misunderstood and misappropriated this gift. Thank you for our ordained clergy people and all the gifts they bring to the body of Christ. Come, Holy Spirit, and awaken the rest of the body; the vast and uncounted men and women who don't see themselves as full court players in the kingdom. Unleash this sleeping giant for the sake of the world. Start with us. We pray in Jesus' name, amen.

The Questions

- When Paul talks about calling in this text, he means first and foremost the calling to belong completely to Jesus Christ, which is lived out in a fruitful life of following him with a winsome, wholehearted obedience. Have you heard that calling? Have you answered it? Have you come to grips with the fact that you are called to be a player rather than a spectator or even a helpful volunteer on the sidelines? What would it look like for you to live out that primary calling in your present vocational role or station in life? What would doubling down in your discipleship mean at this stage in the game for you?

The Most Important Question for Married Couples and Couples Considering Marriage

25

1 CORINTHIANS 7:32–40 | I would like you to be free from concern. An unmarried man is concerned about the Lord's affairs—how he can please the Lord. But a married man is

concerned about the affairs of this world—how he can please his wife—and his interests are divided. An unmarried woman or virgin is concerned about the Lord's affairs: Her aim is to be devoted to the Lord in both body and spirit. But a married woman is concerned about the affairs of this world—how she can please her husband. I am saying this for your own good, not to restrict you, but that you may live in a right way in undivided devotion to the Lord.

If anyone is worried that he might not be acting honorably toward the virgin he is engaged to, and if his passions are too strong and he feels he ought to marry, he should do as he wants. He is not sinning. They should get married. But the man who has settled the matter in his own mind, who is under no compulsion but has control over his own will, and who has made up his mind not to marry the virgin—this man also does the right thing. So then, he who marries the virgin does right, but he who does not marry her does better.

A woman is bound to her husband as long as he lives. But if her husband dies, she is free to marry anyone she wishes, but he must belong to the Lord. In my judgment, she is happier if she stays as she is—and I think that I too have the Spirit of God.

Consider This

To those sanctified in Christ Jesus and called to be his holy people (i.e., us):

As you have noticed by now, throughout this letter in particular, Paul shifts in and out of different voices or points of view. At times, he claims the inspiration of the Holy Spirit and the authority of God in his holdings. At other times, he owns his counsel as his own opinion and is careful to qualify it as such. In today's text, Paul gets at the rationale behind his counsel to Christians to remain unmarried if possible, which he did not claim as the Lord's counsel. Here's the bottom line:

I am saying this for your own good, not to restrict you, but that you may live in a right way in undivided devotion to the Lord.

The big discipleship issue for Paul is developing an "undivided devotion to the Lord." I have always appreciated the succinctness of the way the psalmist puts this idea. I'd encourage you to commit this prayer to the memory of your heart and pray it often. "Teach me your way, O Lord, that I may walk in your truth; give me an undivided heart to revere your name" (Ps. 86:11 NRSV).

Do married people necessarily have a divided heart when it comes to their devotion to the Lord? No. Do single people necessarily have an undivided heart when it comes to the Lord? No. In today's and prior day's texts, Paul is doing at least two things. On the one hand, he's lifting the calling of celibacy as a legitimate way of serving the ministry of the gospel. In fact, it is Paul's personal preference as evidenced by his own life and teaching. On the other hand, he raises the bar on marriage. He does this primarily through his authoritative teaching on divorce and remarriage. In all of it, Paul seems to counsel that if one is considering marriage, it's a good choice but the most critical choice is *whom* to marry.

There are many questions that must be asked and explored in the discernment process of whether two people should marry or not, but one question towers above the rest. Will this person tend to aid you in cultivating and maintaining an undivided devotion to the Lord? Is this a person you can encourage and aid to maintain an undivided devotion to the Lord? It's also a great intervening question to explore for those who are already married. Are you contributing to your spouse's development of an undivided attention to the Lord or distracting from it? If change needs to happen on that front, how might it come about?

Both marriage and celibacy are exceedingly challenging callings and both are filled with good gifts. One is not to be elevated over the other in the kingdom of God, but both should be celebrated, honored, and affirmed. That said, I will end today with one of my favorite quotes on marriage from Tertullian, a leader of the church in the third century:

> How beautiful, then, the marriage of two Christians, two who are one in hope, one in desire, one in the way of life they follow, one in the religion they practice. They are as brother and sister, both servants of the same Master. Nothing divides them, either in flesh or in spirit. They are, in very truth, two in one flesh; and where there is but one flesh there is also but one spirit. They pray together, they worship together, they fast together; instructing one another, encouraging one another, strengthening one another. Side by side they

visit God's church and partake of God's Banquet; side by side they face difficulties and persecution, share their consolations. They have no secrets from one another; they never shun each other's company; they never bring sorrow to each other's hearts. Unembarrassed they visit the sick and assist the needy. They give alms without anxiety; they attend the Sacrifice without difficulty; they perform their daily exercises of piety without hindrance. They need not be furtive about making the Sign of the Cross, nor timorous in greeting the brethren, nor silent in asking a blessing of God. Psalms and hymns they sing to one another, striving to see which one of them will chant more beautifully the praises of their Lord. Hearing and seeing this, Christ rejoices. To such as these He gives His peace. Where there are two together, there also He is present; and where He is, there evil is not. (*The Beauty of Christian Marriage*)

The Prayer

Our Father in heaven, hallowed be your name. Your kingdom come. Your will be done, on earth as it is in heaven. I agree with the psalmist in the prayer, "Teach me your way, O LORD, that I may walk in your truth; give me an undivided heart to revere your name." Come, Holy Spirit, and help me to understand the fullness of the calling you have placed on my life and make every provision necessary that it might be fulfilled. I want to do your will, Lord. In Jesus' name, amen.

The Questions

- What is the present quality of your life before the Lord? Picture a spectrum with "Distracted" at the left end and "Undivided" at the right end. Where do you put yourself along the spectrum as relates to your relationship with God today? How can you take a small step today to reunite your heart before the Lord? It's another way of asking, What might repentance look like? Another way of asking it would be, What in your present way of life needs to be realigned to move you toward an undivided devotion to Jesus Christ? How might you encourage married couples in light of today's text? How might you encourage persons considering marriage? How might you encourage single people who are considering the calling of celibacy?

26 | Until My Rights Are More about You than Me, They Are Wrongs

1 CORINTHIANS 8:1–13 | Now about food sacrificed to idols: We know that "We all possess knowledge." But knowledge puffs up while love builds up. Those who think they know something do not yet know as they ought to know. But whoever loves God is known by God.

So then, about eating food sacrificed to idols: We know that "An idol is nothing at all in the world" and that "There is no

God but one." For even if there are so-called gods, whether in heaven or on earth (as indeed there are many "gods" and many "lords"), yet for us there is but one God, the Father, from whom all things came and for whom we live; and there is but one Lord, Jesus Christ, through whom all things came and through whom we live.

But not everyone possesses this knowledge. Some people are still so accustomed to idols that when they eat sacrificial food they think of it as having been sacrificed to a god, and since their conscience is weak, it is defiled. But food does not bring us near to God; we are no worse if we do not eat, and no better if we do.

Be careful, however, that the exercise of your rights does not become a stumbling block to the weak. For if someone with a weak conscience sees you, with all your knowledge, eating in an idol's temple, won't that person be emboldened to eat what is sacrificed to idols? So this weak brother or sister, for whom Christ died, is destroyed by your knowledge. When you sin against them in this way and wound their weak conscience, you sin against Christ. Therefore, if what I eat causes my brother or sister to fall into sin, I will never eat meat again, so that I will not cause them to fall.

Consider This

To those sanctified in Christ Jesus and called to be his holy people (i.e., us):

Today's text holds a teaching of profound and universal importance for the followers of Jesus. The problem with today's text is we have no clearly comparable situation in the twenty-first century (at least in the United States) in which to make application of the text. We have many challenges as Christians today, but eating meat sacrificed to idols is not one of them. Because the big idea here is the issue of a Christian doing something that causes another to stumble, people immediately want to jump to issues of a Christian's use of alcohol in a world filled with alcoholics. There is application in this instance to be sure, but this discussion will be more properly had in chapter 10. Stay tuned. For now, today's text presents us a much bigger principle which cuts to the heart of the Christian faith.

We know that "We all possess knowledge." But knowledge puffs up while love builds up. Those who think they know something do not yet know as they ought to know. But whoever loves God is known by God.

The Corinthians were all about wisdom and knowledge. The big problem and the ironic sign that they possessed neither of them is the way they sought to distinguish themselves over and against others who did not possess such wisdom and knowledge. Their knowledge produced a kind of elitism among them. It puffed them up. They readily translated their so-called knowledge into their own individual freedoms and rights without regard to the way their exercising those freedoms and rights would impact others.

Despite the way texts like these often get misappropriated into anti-intellectual sentiment in the church, knowledge is not bad. The issue is how we appropriate knowledge. Does our knowledge lead us to a deeper knowing of others or does it lead us to pride in ourselves?

Those who think they know something do not yet know as they ought to know.

I'll close with an analogy that may turn out to be a rabbit trail through a minefield, but as an attorney I can't resist it. While the Constitution of the United States is a brilliant document, the real genius came in the Bill of Rights. The problem with the Bill of Rights, though, is we forget the over-arching purpose. The Bill of Rights was not established to create a national ethos of unfettered individual freedom to justify doing just about everything under the sun under the auspices of one's individual rights regardless of the offense or injury it may cause to others. The Bill of Rights was established to protect the citizenry from the government. Freedom of speech and freedom of religion and the right to bear arms and to be free from unreasonable search and seizure and so forth are not meant to establish a totalizing individual autonomy. They are meant to foster the common good and a government by the people for the people.

Free speech has nothing to do with a sacrilegious art display or an expletive on my T-shirt, and everything to do with the ability to voice a contrary opinion about the president of the United States without being arrested for it. These rights are for the flourishing and preservation of a certain kind of community. They are for the sake of one another far more than for my individual ability to do whatever the heck I want to do. We have run far amuck of our founders' intentions because these rights have become far more about ourselves as individuals than our relationships with one another. We think we know something, but do not yet know as we ought to know.

The issue is not our rights but our relationships. The issue is not knowledge of the law but knowing one another. We have not been rescued and set free from sin for freedom's sake but for the love of God and the love of neighbor. Until my rights are more about you than they are about me then they are really wrongs.

The Prayer

Our Father in heaven, hallowed be your name. Your kingdom come. Your will be done, on earth as it is in heaven. Yes, Lord, knowledge is good but love is infinitely better. I ask you for the gift of the humility of Jesus, to have the mind of Christ, that I might learn to handle knowledge with love. I confess my pride as sin; even more I confess that most of my pride is yet hidden from me. Come, Holy Spirit, and gently reveal my pride and give me the grace to repent. I pray in Jesus' name, amen.

The Questions

- Where do you see this knowledge versus love conflict in your relationships? In your life? How do you relate to this distinction between individual rights and the good of others?

The Difference between Being a Doormat and a Doorway

27

1 CORINTHIANS 9:1–12 | Am I not free? Am I not an apostle? Have I not seen Jesus our Lord? Are you not the result of my work in the Lord? Even though I may not be an apostle to others, surely I am to you! For you are the seal of my apostleship in the Lord.

This is my defense to those who sit in judgment on me. Don't we have the right to food and drink? Don't we have the right to take a believing wife along with us, as do the other apostles and the Lord's brothers and Cephas? Or is it only I and Barnabas who lack the right to not work for a living?

Who serves as a soldier at his own expense? Who plants a vineyard and does not eat its grapes? Who tends a flock and does not drink the milk? Do I say this merely on human authority? Doesn't the Law say the same thing? For it is written in the Law of Moses: "Do not muzzle an ox while it is treading out the grain." Is it about oxen that God is concerned? Surely he says this for us, doesn't he? Yes, this was written for us, because whoever plows and threshes should be able to do so in the hope of sharing in the harvest. If we have sown spiritual seed among you, is it too much if we reap a material harvest from you? If others have this right of support from you, shouldn't we have it all the more?

But we did not use this right. On the contrary, we put up with anything rather than hinder the gospel of Christ.

Consider This

To those sanctified in Christ Jesus and called to be his holy people (i.e., us):

There's a complex argument here, but a simple case. I'll cut to the chase. Remember Paul's admonition to the Corinthians not to do something just because they could or had the right to do it? The real issue is how the exercise of their rights would impact other people. Here's how I put it: until my rights are more about you than they are about me, they are really wrongs.

Christians are all about rights when it comes to the defending and protecting the rights of others, but not so much when it comes to asserting their own. We don't have to spend our energy standing up for ourselves because we have a High Priest in the heavens who stands up for us. Because of that, we can spend our energy standing up for others, taking care of others, protecting others, and all for the sake of the gospel of Jesus Christ.

At least we can say this is Paul's "way of life in Christ Jesus." Paul's chief concern is for others to hear the gospel, and he knows that nothing stops up the ears of hearers more than a disconnect between what a person says and what they actually do. In today's text, Paul lays out his case with lawyerly precision. Paul was not accepting any kind of remuneration from the Corinthians for his ministry in their midst. Rather than admiring this approach, they chose to use it as evidence in their case to attack Paul's legitimacy as an apostle. In other words, they interpreted his refusal to accept compensation as his own admission that he was not an apostle (i.e., "Of course he's not taking our money—he knows he has no right to it!").

Paul was on the verge of being infuriated. Verses 9–12 roll out one zinger after another. Here he is doing something completely benevolent for their sake and they turn around and attack him. There's an old adage that floats around the church that seems apropos here: "Sheep bite!" But you've got to love how Paul gives the closing argument here:

But we did not use this right. On the contrary, we put up with anything rather than hinder the gospel of Christ.

As the apostle rests his case, he shows us what real maturity in Christ looks like. It's not about me. It's about Jesus, and because it's all about Jesus, it's all about you. Right here we see the love of God and neighbor in perfect harmony, and he's able to do it without gritting his teeth or grinning and bearing it because he knows that he knows that he knows in his deepest, innermost self how high and how long and how deep and how wide is the love of Christ Jesus for him, and this love constrains and compels him to not just talk about it to others but to demonstrate it. This is the mind of Christ operative in Paul—as Thomas à Kempis would put it, "the royal way of the holy Cross."

That's a high calling, my friends, and it is our calling. It's not about being a doormat but becoming a genuine doorway into the heart of Jesus. No, it's about Jesus himself, the door, revealing the humble way into the kingdom of God in and through us.

The Prayer

Our Father in heaven, hallowed be your name. Your kingdom come. Your will be done, on earth as it is in heaven. I confess, Lord, I struggle to put up with much of anything. I am all too ready to complain and criticize and push back when I am offended. Teach me that the way of the cross is the way of bearing offense. Come, Holy Spirit, and show me that to be offended merely reveals my pride. Give me the grace to walk in the way of Jesus, who returns good for bad. In his name I pray, amen.

The Questions

- Do you struggle with this notion of not asserting our own rights but instead standing for the rights of others? Are you grasping the difference between being a doormat for others to walk on and a doorway which others can walk through? Have you ever found yourself bearing reproach for the sake of Jesus? Do you see the fine line between what Paul is doing here and stepping over the line into self-righteousness?

Dealing with the Other Golden Rule

28

1 CORINTHIANS 9:13–18 | Don't you know that those who serve in the temple get their food from the temple, and that those who serve at the altar share in what is offered on the altar? In the same way, the Lord has commanded that those who preach the gospel should receive their living from the gospel.

But I have not used any of these rights. And I am not writing this in the hope that you will do such things for me, for I would rather die than allow anyone to deprive me of this boast. For when I preach the gospel, I cannot boast, since I am compelled to preach. Woe to me if I do not preach the gospel! If I preach voluntarily, I have a reward; if not voluntarily, I am simply discharging the trust committed to me. What then is my reward? Just this: that in preaching the gospel I may offer it free of charge, and so not make full use of my rights as a preacher of the gospel.

Consider This

To those sanctified in Christ Jesus and called to be his holy people (i.e., us):

Today's text brings to mind the other golden rule. You know the one I'm talking about. "He or she who has the gold makes the rule." Let's recall what's going on here in Corinth. Paul has made these people mad. He's put the kibbutz on the prostitutes and all the socializing over meals in the pagan temples. We would do well now to remind ourselves of the salutation in this letter—the one we reprint every day at the top of the entry: To those sanctified in Christ Jesus and called to be his holy people (i.e., us).

Paul is preaching the gospel of Jesus Christ and making disciples, which entails some fairly dramatic change in this community of Corinthians. Because they were not appreciating his challenges to them, they played the money card—sort of. The problem is they couldn't control Paul with money. Paul didn't have a problem with money or taking money for doing the work of the gospel—until it was a problem. And I think he knew it would pose a problem in Corinth. He was right. The bottom line for Paul is he would not allow himself to become beholden to anyone but Jesus Christ. In fact, that's what "Jesus Christ is Lord" meant for Paul, period. He would be beholden to no one else, which is another way of saying he was free to serve with no strings attached.

Paul was going to preach the gospel to this church he started whether they respected him as an apostle or not, whether they paid him or not, whether they received his counsel and heeded his warnings or not.

Woe to me if I do not preach the gospel! If I preach voluntarily, I have a reward; if not voluntarily, I am simply discharging the trust committed to me. What then is my reward? Just this: that in preaching the gospel I may offer it free of charge, and so not make full use of my rights as a preacher of the gospel.

The Prayer

Our Father in heaven, hallowed be your name. Your kingdom come. Your will be done, on earth as it is in heaven. Thank you for the ways you call me to have a humble heart, an undivided heart, and an uncompromising obedience. To be called is not enough, Lord. I need to be empowered. Come, Holy Spirit, and fill my willingness with the power of your willingness. I cannot be like you apart from you. In Jesus' name, amen.

The Questions

- Does this kind of thing happen today? You tell me. Do preachers not preach on the hard things because they fear offending people who have resources? Have you ever been around people who try to leverage their giving in potentially manipulative ways? Have you ever been one of those people?

Baby, You Were Born to Run—Just Not like You Thought

29

1 CORINTHIANS 9:19–27 | Though I am free and belong to no one, I have made myself a slave to everyone, to win as many as possible. To the Jews I became like a Jew, to win the Jews. To those under the law I became like one under the law (though

I myself am not under the law), so as to win those under the law. To those not having the law I became like one not having the law (though I am not free from God's law but am under Christ's law), so as to win those not having the law. To the weak I became weak, to win the weak. I have become all things to all people so that by all possible means I might save some. I do all this for the sake of the gospel, that I may share in its blessings.

Do you not know that in a race all the runners run, but only one gets the prize? Run in such a way as to get the prize. Everyone who competes in the games goes into strict training. They do it to get a crown that will not last, but we do it to get a crown that will last forever. Therefore I do not run like someone running aimlessly; I do not fight like a boxer beating the air. No, I strike a blow to my body and make it my slave so that after I have preached to others, I myself will not be disqualified for the prize.

Consider This

To those sanctified in Christ Jesus and called to be his holy people (i.e., us):

Today we get to a bumper sticker text. You know what I mean. It's the stuff of refrigerator magnets: "Run in such a way as to get the prize." It typically gets interpreted to mean such things as run faster, try harder, and you can do better. "Eyes on the Prize" the T-shirt might say.

This is typically how the Christian faith gets pitched. It comes down to human efforts to be more disciplined and an athletic striving to be more spiritual. A person can run a thousand miles in this direction before ever realizing the Christian faith is not a race. Read it again.

Do you not know that in a race all the runners run, but only one gets the prize? Run in such a way as to get the prize.

The Christian faith is not a race. It is about a prize. The Christian faith is about running with focus, not running faster. It's not about precise form, but perfect freedom.

Let's take the text off of the T-shirt and remember the biblical context. Paul has been exhorting the Corinthians to leave behind their former way of life and to enter into the new life to which they have been called—the calling to be God's holy people. To be clear, holiness does not mean religious behavior. It means something more like living in the zone, the place of glorious aliveness in the power of the Holy Spirit. This zone of the Holy Spirit–empowered life is much more like playing a game than grinding it out.

I have a sense these Christians in Corinth had lost sight of the big picture. All they could see was the salacious, seductive culture all around them. When we lose sight of the grand vision, we tend to succumb to the closest thing we can see. Remember when the freed Hebrew slaves wanted to go back to Egypt? They had lost sight of the vision. There's a verse in Proverbs that says, "Where there is no vision, the people perish" (29:18 KJV). This text is a favorite of leaders who want people to follow their particular vision. That's not what it means. It's about *the vision*—the vision of God that has been revealed to us in Jesus Christ. Another common misunderstanding of the Christian faith comes when we think the prize is somehow at the end. If we run faster and try harder now, we will surely win the prize at the end when we die or even later at the resurrection of the dead. To be sure, those will be major prize-winning days, but this is not what Paul is talking about.

For Paul, and for us, the prize is Jesus. Because Jesus Christ has risen from the dead and ascended to the right hand of God and sent the promised Holy Spirit, the prize now exists in the present—right now. Paul is not hoping for a good outcome in the future. It's hard to grasp this concept, but Paul is living in the present—from the future. To "run in such a way as to get the prize" means to live fully in the freedom of the Holy Spirit—right now, so much so that the grace of Jesus Christ becomes the palpable goodness of your everyday life and the life of Jesus becomes the power of your love for God and neighbor.

Paul is waving his arms about trying to get our attention as if to say, "People of God, this is *real*. This is now. Stop wasting your life on all of these things that promise life but only deliver death. Run in the new way of the Spirit. Run in the unconventional way of the cross. Run in the un-wearying way of the power of God."

The Prayer

Our Father in heaven, hallowed be your name. Your kingdom come. Your will be done, on earth as it is in heaven. I am ready to lay down all my striving to run faster. I want to run instead with ever-deepening focus. Come, Holy Spirit, and help me run in the new way of the Spirit. Help me run in the unconventional way of the cross. Show me how to run in the un-wearying way of the power of God. I pray in Jesus' name, amen.

The Questions

• Have you settled for a sophisticated substitute version of a prosperous life instead of the *real life* that comes through knowing Jesus Christ in the power of the Holy Spirit now? It's critically important to be honest with yourself. Have you accepted a version of the Christian faith that is more about trying harder to not sin and to do better, grinding it out, and hoping it will all turn out okay in the end? Are you ready to take the next step to "run in such a way as to get the prize"? Are you ready in a new way to exchange your old life for the new creation?

Why Those Who Cannot Remember Their Past Are Destined to Repeat It

30

1 CORINTHIANS 10:1–13 | For I do not want you to be ignorant of the fact, brothers and sisters, that our ancestors were all under the cloud and that they all passed through the sea. They were all baptized into Moses in the cloud and in the sea. They all ate the same spiritual food and drank the same spiritual

drink; for they drank from the spiritual rock that accompanied them, and that rock was Christ. Nevertheless, God was not pleased with most of them; their bodies were scattered in the wilderness.

Now these things occurred as examples to keep us from setting our hearts on evil things as they did. Do not be idolaters, as some of them were; as it is written: "The people sat down to eat and drink and got up to indulge in revelry." We should not commit sexual immorality, as some of them did—and in one day twenty-three thousand of them died. We should not test Christ, as some of them did—and were killed by snakes. And do not grumble, as some of them did—and were killed by the destroying angel.

These things happened to them as examples and were written down as warnings for us, on whom the culmination of the ages has come. So, if you think you are standing firm, be careful that you don't fall! No temptation has overtaken you except what is common to mankind. And God is faithful; he will not let you be tempted beyond what you can bear. But when you are tempted, he will also provide a way out so that you can endure it.

Consider This

To those sanctified in Christ Jesus and called to be his holy people (i.e., us):

These things happened to them as examples and were written down as warnings for us, on whom the culmination of the ages has come.

This sentence explodes with implications. Let's list them:

1. History is not in the past. Sure, history is historical—as in it happened in the past—but when God intervenes in history it has implications for all eternity.

2. When Paul says "our ancestors" to the Corinthians, he is telling Gentiles that they now have Hebrew ancestors. He is also telling them that because of Jesus, the biblical story of creation, fall, flood, Israel, and exile is now their living, breathing story. In other words, the story of the Old Testament is their past even though it did not actually happen to them. He means that in order to be God's holy people, we must increasingly understand and embrace God's holy history. Why?

3. Because "these things happened to them as examples and were written down as warnings for us, on whom the culmination of the ages has come."

4. Paul is not moralizing with the rules here. He is telling them the story without which they will be lost in the midst of the world of Corinth. In this case, it's the story of Egypt, slavery, Passover, deliverance, Red Sea, wilderness, testing, and so on.

5. It cannot be overstated. The Old Testament is not an elective in the catalog of Christian discipleship. It is a core-required course. In fact, it's really a pre-requisite course to the New Testament. Because most of us (i.e., Gentiles) come to the faith through a first exposure to the New Testament, the required, pre-requisite course in the Old Testament can be easily neglected. (It's kind of like picking up your favorite television show in its final season and thinking you've pretty much gotten the story.)

So don't tell me, "God will make a way when there seems to be no way." Tell me the story where God made a way when there was no way. Tell me the against-all-odds story of Moses and the Red Sea. I need the textured grit of the whole true story in order to understand my own situation in twenty-first-century Corinthian America. We aren't the first generation to deal with insurmountable odds and overwhelming temptation. Without remembering our bigger story and those who have preceded us and the God who goes ahead of us and comes behind us and literally hems us in, we are destined to make the same predictable mistakes and repeat a past from which we have been gloriously delivered.

The Prayer

Our Father in heaven, hallowed be your name. Your kingdom come. Your will be done, on earth as it is in heaven. Thank you for the treasure of your Word, which tells us our story in exquisite detail. Increase my appetite to know this story, inside out and upside down. Though I have learned so much, my understanding remains far too thin. Come, Holy Spirit, and help me become a person of one book. In Jesus' name, amen.

The Questions

- So where are you with your *big story*? How well are you remembering the first three-fourths of your Bible? What keeps you from digging into the Old Testament? Admittedly, it's a challenge, but what in particular challenges you?

What's a next step you can take to turn away from your ignorance or indifference or whatever it is in order to go to the next place of biblical understanding and as a consequence, Holy Spirit–filled faith?

Is Jesus like You?

31

1 CORINTHIANS 10:25–11:1 | Eat anything sold in the meat market without raising questions of conscience, for, "The earth is the Lord's, and everything in it."

If an unbeliever invites you to a meal and you want to go, eat whatever is put before you without raising questions of conscience. But if someone says to you, "This has been offered in sacrifice," then do not eat it, both for the sake of the one who told you and for the sake of conscience. I am referring to the other person's conscience, not yours. For why is my freedom being judged by another's conscience? If I take part in the meal with thankfulness, why am I denounced because of something I thank God for?

So whether you eat or drink or whatever you do, do it all for the glory of God. Do not cause anyone to stumble, whether Jews, Greeks or the church of God—even as I try to please everyone in every way. For I am not seeking my own good but the good of many, so that they may be saved.

Follow my example, as I follow the example of Christ.

Consider This

To those sanctified in Christ Jesus and called to be his holy people (i.e., us):

Jesus was like Paul. It sounds strange to say, but that would be the goal for all of our lives; for someone to say to someone else of us, "Jesus was like Tim or Julie or Bob or Jane." I picked up this notion from the late great British theologian and apologist, G. K. Chesterton. In his book on St. Francis of Assisi (which I heartily recommend), he offered this rationale.

> Now in truth while it has always seemed natural to explain St. Francis in the light of Christ, it has not occurred to many people to explain Christ in the light of St. Francis. Perhaps the word "light" is not here the proper metaphor; but the same truth is admitted in the accepted metaphor of the mirror. St. Francis is the mirror of Christ rather as the moon is the mirror of the sun. The moon is much smaller than the sun, but it is also much nearer to us; and being less vivid it is more visible. Exactly in the same sense St. Francis is nearer to us, and being a mere man like ourselves is in that sense more imaginable.

Recall that we wrestled with those excruciatingly difficult two words we are so reticent to say, "Imitate me."

Can I cut to the chase today? The truth is people are following your example. People are imitating you, whether you like it or not. Where is your life leading them? Is your life leading others to discover the goodness of God our Father, the grace of Jesus Christ, the power of the Holy Spirit, the joy of the kingdom of God in the midst of the most difficult trial? There's only one way to answer yes to this and that is if you are actively discovering and experiencing these realities in an ongoing, everyday way.

Whose example are you following who is following the example of Christ? Who are you imitating? Without someone to imitate, with skin on, in our day in and day out lives, faith easily morphs into an ethereal idealism that, at best, stays in our heads and, at worst, remains on the pages of our Bibles.

The Prayer

Our Father in heaven, hallowed be your name. Your kingdom come. Your will be done, on earth as it is in heaven. It seems like a stretch, and maybe just a dream, but it would be something for someone to say Jesus was like me. Come, Holy Spirit, and make it so, for only you can. I pray in Jesus' name, amen.

The Questions

- Let's get beyond rhetorical questions and really ask: Whose examples are you following who are following the example of Christ? Who do you think is following your example (for better or for worse)? What are some concrete ways your life can follow the example of Christ? What is his example?

32 Why Facebook Now Offers Unlimited Customized Gender Identity Options (for Americans)

1 CORINTHIANS 11:2–16 | I praise you for remembering me in everything and for holding to the traditions just as I passed them on to you. But I want you to realize that the head of every man is Christ, and the head of the woman is man, and the head of Christ is God. Every man who prays or prophesies with his head covered dishonors his head. But every woman who prays or prophesies with her head uncovered dishonors her head—it is the same as having her head shaved. For if a woman does not cover her head, she might as well have her hair cut off; but if it is a disgrace for a woman to have her hair cut off or her head shaved, then she should cover her head.

A man ought not to cover his head, since he is the image and glory of God; but woman is the glory of man. For man did not come from woman, but woman from man; neither was man created for woman, but woman for man. It is for this reason that a woman ought to have authority over her own head, because of the angels. Nevertheless, in the Lord woman is not independent of man, nor is man independent of woman. For as woman came from man, so also man is born of woman. But everything comes from God.

Judge for yourselves: Is it proper for a woman to pray to God with her head uncovered? Does not the very nature of things teach you that if a man has long hair, it is a disgrace to him, but that if a woman has long hair, it is her glory? For long hair is given to her as a covering. If anyone wants to be contentious about this, we have no other practice—nor do the churches of God.

Consider This

To those sanctified in Christ Jesus and called to be his holy people (i.e., us):

This is perhaps the most challenging passage in the letter to properly interpret because it is so laden with first-century cultural and contextual issues, which are, for all practical purposes, impossible to competently interpret and confidently understand. As a result, where there is a vacuum of understanding, the proliferation of interpretations abound.

Perhaps the main way this text has been interpreted through the centuries is with respect to authority relationships between men and women. Because I am an elf among giants in the realm of biblical interpreters who have taken on this text through the ages, I will tread with great caution in any assertions I make, and stay close to the holdings of my trusted teachers.

1. First, note the only use of the word authority (*exousia* in Greek) comes in verse 10 and relates to a woman's authority over her own head.

2. All of Paul's usage of "head" terminology has nothing to do with "authority," or else he would have used "authority" language to articulate it, as he did in verse 10.

3. Gender matters. This issue of the covering or not covering the head and with respect to one's hair has to do with the apparent blurring of gender distinctions going on in ancient Corinth. Paul's effort here is to sort that out in the terms of theology and relationship rather than of power and authority.

4. The relationships intended by God between men and women are not framed in terms of hierarchy and subordination but in the framework of mutual submission. (*Nevertheless, in the Lord woman is not independent of man, nor is man independent of woman. For as woman came from man, so also man is born of woman.*)

5. In this ancient context, public worship served as a venue where these complexities were symbolically signed and demonstrated. The issue Paul seems to get at is that gender distinctions matter not with respect to power and authority but as relates to the glory of God. There exists an undeniable complementary distinctiveness between men and women, but this distinctiveness is not meant to construct relationships on a hierarchical power-oriented framework. It is meant to shape complementary, interdependent, mutually submissive relationships to the end of demonstrating the glory of God.

6. For Paul, the big, massive, overarching, and overwhelming deal here is God. As he puts it, "But everything comes from God."

It strikes me that today's text, as convoluted as it may seem based on two thousand years of cultural, geographical, and linguistic differences, holds immense importance for our twenty-first-century context. As a person who grew up and came of age in the benign surroundings of a late twentieth-century small town in Arkansas, to say the world has changed seems a profound understatement. Then again, maybe from even before first-century Corinth these issues have always been as present and confoundingly sophisticated as they seem to be now. I grew up with a fairly simple understanding that when the Bible said, "male and female he created them," it meant "male and female he created them." In 2014, Facebook relented from their prior fifty-eight pre-selected gender options and now permits unlimited gender identity classifications for its United States–based users who lodged the complaint.

It strikes me that a well-placed, "Toto, I've a feeling we're not in Kansas anymore" assertion would fit well here.

In the end, it comes down to a choice between the worldview shaped by the biblical vision of God's kingdom and all the other worldviews being socially constructed and advanced as we speak, all of which are mere variations on the broken legacy of Genesis 3. It may seem like an oversimplification, but underneath the catastrophe of the so-called sexual revolution and the radical feminist movements of the 1960s are gross misunderstandings and egregious misappropriations of the Bible. Human sexuality is a good gift. Feminism is a good gift. Unfortunately, both have been radicalized by the ancient rebellion against God and have led not only to the tragic distortion of God's creation but to all manner of reactionary biblical interpretations by the church itself in response, sadly—including our haircuts.

The only way forward is a return to the fundamental realities of the humble people of God immersed in the world of the Word of God and the Spirit of God which alone advance the will of God—which is nothing short of the gospel of the kingdom of the God and Father of our Lord Jesus Christ.

The Prayer

Our Father in heaven, hallowed be your name. Your kingdom come. Your will be done, on earth as it is in heaven. Thank you for the clarity of Scripture, especially in the midst of this age of confusion we now inhabit. Come, Holy Spirit, and give us compassion and great patience for the broken and confused. More so, give us the kind of love that can endure being disdained and dismissed for daring to believe in the simple clarity of your Word. We pray in the name of Jesus, amen.

The Questions

- While we can't put the toothpaste back in the tube (in a manner of speaking), we can gather ourselves as God's people around the fundamental practices of Bible study and Holy Spirit faith formation. How are you going about that now? Are you becoming a real student of Scripture? Or is it a nice devotional habit for you? Does rigorous biblical formation still seem optional to you; a nice add-on? Or is your life coming to depend on it? What would it take to up your game? Are you willing to make that change and investment?

What If We Tailgated before Church?

33

1 CORINTHIANS 11:17–26 | In the following directives I have no praise for you, for your meetings do more harm than good. In the first place, I hear that when you come together as a church, there are divisions among you, and to some extent I believe it. No doubt there have to be differences among you to show which of you have God's approval. So then, when you come together, it is not the Lord's Supper you eat, for when you are eating, some of you go ahead with your own private suppers. As a result, one person remains hungry and another gets drunk. Don't you have homes to eat and drink in? Or do you despise the church of God by humiliating those who have nothing? What shall I say to you? Shall I praise you? Certainly not in this matter!

For I received from the Lord what I also passed on to you: The Lord Jesus, on the night he was betrayed, took bread, and when he had given thanks, he broke it and said, "This is my body, which is for you; do this in remembrance of me." In the same way, after supper he took the cup, saying, "This cup is the new covenant in my blood; do this, whenever you drink it, in remembrance of me." For whenever you eat this bread and drink this cup, you proclaim the Lord's death until he comes.

Consider This

To those sanctified in Christ Jesus and called to be his holy people (i.e., us):

Worship matters to God, and not just *that* we worship but *how* we worship. I don't so much mean how we worship with respect to guitars or organs, but with respect to order. Paul will spend the next few chapters of his letter dealing with the issue of order in worship for the Corinthian church. And he's not happy about what he's heard.

This issue he raises regarding the Lord's Supper is an interesting one and can seem a long way from our situation today. A closer look might reveal a different story. In order to make my point, let me describe what they were doing then in a more contemporary analogy.

Imagine that the church tailgated in the parking lot before worship. First, get a picture of the sweet fleet of vehicles gracing the place; lots of Range Rovers and Mercedes SUVs, several Porsche Cayenne Turbo SUVs, tons of F-150 pickup trucks and tricked-out minivans. Now imagine the incredible display of grills and cookers and accessories that come with today's standard tailgate. Then get a load of the incredible buffet of food—steaks, burgers, ribs, pulled pork, bratwursts and all manner of boutique hotdogs, potato salad, coleslaw, relish trays, and we haven't even gotten to dessert yet.

Visualize the party people going from tailgate to tailgate sampling food and saying hello and yes, imbibing the variety of libations.

Worship is about to begin, but there's a small problem. All the folks who don't have fancy rides, elaborate tailgate gear, and endless food begin showing up for worship. Most of them rode a bus for hours to get there. By the time they could get to the tailgate at which they would get nothing to eat, the tailgaters are already in church and helping themselves to the Lord's Supper. Not only did they not wait for the poor people who were late, they snarfed up all of the provisions for the Lord's Supper and drank up the remaining wine until they could hardly walk out of the building and find their cars.

This gives us something of a mildly analogous snapshot of what was going on in the church at Corinth. Consider the mockery this was making of the Lord's Supper itself. Paul suggested that they couldn't even legitimately call what they were doing the Lord's Supper.

So then, when you come together, it is not the Lord's Supper you eat, for when you are eating, some of you go ahead with your own private suppers. As a result, one person remains hungry and another gets drunk.

In some sense, Paul seems to say, "Don't for a minute think you are remembering the Lord when you have practically forgotten the poor. It's not the ritual that creates the righteousness, but the righteousness that verifies the ritual." It's a theme as old as Amos and Isaiah and as new as last Sunday. If we are going to forget our neighbors in need on Monday there's little point in showing up for worship on Sunday, tail-gate or not.

It seems fitting to give a prophet the last word.

> "I hate, I despise your religious festivals; your assemblies are a stench to me. Even though you bring me burnt offerings and grain offerings, I will not accept them. Though you bring choice fellowship offerings, I will have no regard for them. Away with the noise of your songs! I will not listen to the music of your harps. But let justice roll on like a river, righteousness like a never-failing stream!" (Amos 5:21–24)

The mercy of God is that there's still time to take the next step.

The Prayer

Our Father in heaven, hallowed be your name. Your kingdom come. Your will be done, on earth as it is in heaven. This word from Amos challenges me. "Let justice roll on like a river, righteousness like a never-failing stream!" I confess I am all too ready to sing the next song without asking myself the hard questions of justice and righteousness. Come, Holy Spirit, and search my heart, show me all the ways my life offends your sense of justice and the ways my worship might grieve your heart. I pray in the name of Jesus, amen.

The Questions

- What is the connection between the worship of God and the care of the poor? Why do you think God cares that we not just give the poor a handout but actually enter into real relationship with them? Can a community actually be an expression of the New Testament church who has no real relationship with the poor other than charitable giving?

Some Reflections on the Original Happy Meal | 34

1 CORINTHIANS 11:27–34 | So then, whoever eats the bread or drinks the cup of the Lord in an unworthy manner will be guilty of sinning against the body and blood of the Lord. Everyone ought to examine themselves before they eat of the bread and drink from the cup. For those who eat and drink without discerning the body of Christ eat and drink judgment on themselves. That is why many among you are weak and sick, and a number of you have fallen asleep. But if we were more discerning with regard to ourselves, we would not come under such judgment. Nevertheless, when we are judged in this way by the Lord, we are being disciplined so that we will not be finally condemned with the world.

So then, my brothers and sisters, when you gather to eat, you should all eat together. Anyone who is hungry should eat something at home, so that when you meet together it may not result in judgment.

And when I come I will give further directions.

Consider This

To those sanctified in Christ Jesus and called to be his holy people (i.e., us):

Winding our way through this labyrinthine Corinthian culture can itself be disorienting with all its food sacrificed to idols and pagan temples and head coverings and "eschatological women." It's time to rise up above the treeline, get a little altitude, and look down upon ancient Corinth with a bit broader perspective.

So before we get to the text, let me press you on a couple of questions. First, what would you say is the central act of the people of God? Would you define it as mission or prayer or discipleship or evangelism or . . . ? My answer, which I think would be the consensus answer of the church through the ages is worship. The worship of God is the central act of the people of God. It brings up my next question. What would you say is the central act of the worship of the people of God? Would you say it's the reading of the Word of God or preaching or singing or prayer or . . . ? My answer, which I also think would be the consensus answer of the church through the ages is the Lord's Supper.

In these closing lines of chapter 11 we are talking about the central act of the central act of the people of God. It has been called the Last Supper and the Lord's Supper and the Eucharist and Holy Communion among other things. From that first celebration on the last night through the earliest days of the church down all the twisted corridors of history and to the present day, despite differences and divisions, the church has always celebrated the Lord's Supper. While we need not diminish other acts and forms of worship nor those who might disagree, we would do well to heed this word from Paul concerning the practice.*

Everyone ought to examine themselves before they eat of the bread and drink from the cup.

So why does the Lord's Supper matter and mean so much? It is simultaneously a celebration of personal relationship with God and community fellowship with the church of all ages at all times and in all places. It involves the core act of human survival: eating and drinking. In the same way, the supper celebrates the reality of greatest necessity required for human flourishing: communion with the Father, Son, and Holy Spirit. The Last Supper engages our five senses of sight, sound, smell, taste, and touch while at the same time involving the intangible perceptions of the soul and spirit. The experience of the Lord's Supper is a profound expression of the kingdom of God: both concrete and mystical, physical and spiritual, seen and unseen, human and divine—indeed, on earth as it is in heaven. The Lord's Supper demonstrates the holistic "one loaf," "one cup," and "one body" unity of a global communion of profound diversity. In partaking of the meal, one must be served by another; it is an act of giving and receiving. Self-service is an oxymoron when it comes to the worship of God. Bread and wine involve fruits of the miraculous creation of God: grains of wheat and grapes from the vine. The preparation of bread and wine involve the creatively industrious work of divinely fashioned human hands. In the Eucharist, we celebrate the infinite abundance of the presence of God in what is apparently the smallest of portions of provision.

The Lord's Supper is a most powerful yet humble means of the grace of God through the remembrance of Jesus Christ by the powerful presence of the Holy Spirit.

Finally, in the act of celebrating the Lord's Supper we witness the saving grace and miraculous mystery of the cross in the bread and cup: the one who was whole became broken so that the ones who were broken could become whole, and the one who was full became empty so that the ones who were empty could become full.

Glory be to the Father, and to the Son, and to the Holy Spirit. As it was in the beginning, is now and ever shall be; world without end, amen.

*I want to be respectful of the Salvation Army and Quakers who as a matter of conviction do not practice the sacraments of Baptism and the Lord's Supper. They do not despise the practice and they honor the convictions of others, but for their own reasons do not observe them in their worship practices.

The Prayer

Our Father in heaven, hallowed be your name. Your kingdom come. Your will be done, on earth as it is in heaven. You, Jesus, who were whole became broken, so that I who am broken can become whole. Thank you. You, Jesus, who were full, made yourself empty, so that I, who am empty, could become filled with all your fullness. Thank you. Come,

Holy Spirit, and immerse me ever deeper in these deepest mysterious realities of on earth as it is in heaven. In Jesus' name. Amen.

The Questions

- How does this reflection on the manifold mysteries of the Lord's Supper impact you? How would you describe your experience of the Lord's Supper in the past? How will you approach the celebration of the Lord's Supper in the future?

"Jesus Is Lord": From Conviction-less Claim to Core Truth

35

1 CORINTHIANS 12:4–14 | There are different kinds of gifts, but the same Spirit distributes them. There are different kinds of service, but the same Lord. There are different kinds of working, but in all of them and in everyone it is the same God at work.

Now to each one the manifestation of the Spirit is given for the common good. To one there is given through the Spirit a message of wisdom, to another a message of knowledge by means of the same Spirit, to another faith by the same Spirit, to another gifts of healing by that one Spirit, to another miraculous powers, to another prophecy, to another distinguishing between spirits, to another speaking in different kinds of tongues, and to still another the interpretation of tongues. All these are the work of one and the same Spirit, and he distributes them to each one, just as he determines.

Just as a body, though one, has many parts, but all its many parts form one body, so it is with Christ. For we were all baptized by one Spirit so as to form one body—whether Jews or Gentiles, slave or free—and we were all given the one Spirit to drink. Even so the body is not made up of one part but of many.

Consider This

To those sanctified in Christ Jesus and called to be his holy people (i.e., us):

I will always remember the late Ed Robb Jr., a great man of God and an evangelist, from Marshall, Texas. There are many reasons to remember him, but the thing that stands out in my mind is the way he began every sermon I ever heard him preach. He probably began all his sermons this way. He would stand up in the pulpit, look out at the people, and in a deep, bold, declarative voice say, "Jesus is Lord!" Then he would proceed to preach the gospel with a gifted anointing like few preachers I have ever heard.

Jesus called him to be an evangelist and the Holy Spirit gifted him for the work of preaching the gospel. I remember one occasion after he preached, the entire church gathered at the altar, literally hundreds of people—everyone there. The Holy Spirit gifted him with the gift of prophecy, which we will get to in a few days.

Today's text helps me better understand what was going on with the extraordinary ministry of Ed Robb. Paul begins on the topic simply enough.

Now about the gifts of the Spirit, brothers and sisters, I do not want you to be uninformed.

Then he addresses the Corinthians' former ways of worshiping idols as pagans. And then this turn:

Therefore I want you to know that no one who is speaking by the Spirit of God says, "Jesus be cursed," and no one can say, "Jesus is Lord," except by the Holy Spirit.

The work of the Holy Spirit will only occur under the authority of Jesus Christ, who alone is Lord, and to call Jesus, Lord, inescapably identifies ourselves as being subject to his authority. There is a tendency with respect to spiritual gifts for people to claim special status because of them, which will ultimately lead to some form of idolatry. That's what the Corinthians were doing, both the pagans and the Christians. Paul would not have it; hence this clarity about lordship.

The gifts of the Holy Spirit are all about the demonstration of the Holy Spirit whose work is to inhabit human beings in such ways as to glorify Jesus Christ. Remember how Paul put it back in chapter 2? "My message and my preaching were not with wise and persuasive words, but with a demonstration of the Spirit's power, so that your faith might not rest on human wisdom, but on God's power" (1 Cor. 2:4–5).

That's what Ed Robb Jr. was doing in his ministry of preaching by declaring at the outset, "Jesus is Lord." From there he would unashamedly preach the gospel and let the chips fall where they would fall. This was not his show. He would not be responsible for who responded or who did not respond. This was the Holy Spirit's work. This was the ministry of Jesus. This was the power of the gospel, period. And it was powerful.

Sometimes I confuse the empowerment and gifts of the Holy Spirit with my own abilities. How do I know? Because I find myself anxious about how well I'm doing (or not). I connect the outcome to my performance and the approval of others.

The gifts of the Holy Spirit are manifestations and demonstrations of the first and last creed of the church: Jesus is Lord!

Jesus is Lord! It's a comprehensive, all-encompassing claim, not only on our lives, but on all of creation. If I never heard another word Ed Robb said, that would have been enough. I suspect somewhere in the communion of saints, he's joyfully declaring those words today.

The Prayer

Our Father in heaven, hallowed be your name. Your kingdom come. Your will be done, on earth as it is in heaven. I confess it with joy—Jesus is Lord! I want to mean it with all my heart, mind, soul, and strength. There are gaps. Come, Holy Spirit, and fill in the gaps in my own character and maturity. Thank you for grace in the meantime. Train me to be so gracious with others. I pray in Jesus' name, amen.

The Questions

- It's one thing to mouth the words, "Jesus is Lord," and another thing to truly mean them. Where are you with that? How about saying, "Jesus, you are my Lord" as a way of defining yourself and your reality? Say it aloud now to Jesus, so your own ears can hear you say it. What effect did that have? What does that mean to you? What if our experience and exercise of the gifts of the Holy Spirit can never exceed our humble submission to the lordship of Jesus Christ? What might that say about the anemic experience of so many Christians today? What might it say about the chaotic and sometimes crazy ways many Christians carry on in the name of the gifts of the Spirit?

What Our Bodies Can Teach Us about God

36

1 CORINTHIANS 12:15–26 | Now if the foot should say, "Because I am not a hand, I do not belong to the body," it would not for that reason stop being part of the body. And if the ear should say, "Because I am not an eye, I do not belong to the body," it would not for that reason stop being part of the body. If the whole body were an eye, where would the sense of hearing be? If the whole body were an ear, where would the sense of smell be? But in fact God has placed the parts in the body, every one of them, just as he wanted them to be. If they

were all one part, where would the body be? As it is, there are many parts, but one body.

The eye cannot say to the hand, "I don't need you!" And the head cannot say to the feet, "I don't need you!" On the contrary, those parts of the body that seem to be weaker are indispensable, and the parts that we think are less honorable we treat with special honor. And the parts that are unpresentable are treated with special modesty, while our presentable parts need no special treatment. But God has put the body together, giving greater honor to the parts that lacked it, so that there should be no division in the body, but that its parts should have equal concern for each other. If one part suffers, every part suffers with it; if one part is honored, every part rejoices with it.

Consider This

To those sanctified in Christ Jesus and called to be his holy people (i.e., us):

Today's text explains itself quite well. When we go home, we are part of a family. When we go to work, we are part of a team. When we join a civic group or club or organization, we are part of a community. When we pay our taxes or show up to vote, we are part of a citizenry. But when it comes to church—God's holy people—we are a body. It's common to think of church as a family or a team or a community and even as a citizenry when it comes down to the "holy nation" descriptor in Scripture. Church is more than all of these things though, because church is a body: the body of Christ. It's easy to think we get that, and at some level we surely do. It's a metaphor at one level, but at another level the Holy Spirit is revealing a deeper and even more literal meaning.

Again, Paul is dealing with the pagan baggage of the Corinthian Christians. They were all about distinguishing themselves from one another and being more important and more spiritual and knowledgeable and wiser and so forth. From chapter 1 to today's text, it was one big spiritual flexing contest with these folks, and they were as divided as the audience at a Miss America beauty pageant. Now they were using the gifts of the Holy Spirit to claim superior awesome-ness, and a lot of it came down to the gift of tongues, which we will get to later.

Paul would not have it. The Holy Spirit revealed a picture to the church of how he worked in the new creation underway. He called this uber-spiritual bunch to look at the most tangible, physical, ever-present reality in their lives: their own bodies. I bet they hated that. The thing about a human body is the way the extraordinary intricacies of so many different systems work so interdependently, seamlessly, and, in many ways, completely effortlessly.

But God has put the body together, giving greater honor to the parts that lacked it, so that there should be no division in the body, but that its parts should have equal concern for each other.

No other image can simultaneously convey inexhaustible diversity and unsurpassable unity better than that of a human body whose exquisite coordination is guarded and governed by the head. And who made the human body? Bingo! And who is the head? Yep! The physical human body images the God who created it, the perfect union and profound diversity of Father, Son, and Holy Spirit.

As with all metaphors, they can be pushed too far—except this one. I'm not sure this metaphor can ever be exhausted of its meaning. The human body, as the ultimate creation of the Creator God, holds the capacity to reveal more about the nature and character of God than all the stars in the universe combined. Could it be another part of the reason that God became a person, a human being, a body?

This text reveals to us the true nature of our relationships with one another: connected, interrelated, seamlessly put together with incalculable diversity and indivisible unity.

I've read this text hundreds of times and never really seen it. I've just let the words pass through my mind as I told myself, "I get it." I think I am only beginning to barely grasp it. What's different this time? As I typed these words I became aware of the miraculous way my ten fingers did their work—all doing different things yet all doing the same thing—working with a diversity of letters to create a multiplicity of words, each meaning something different yet together making new meaning.

The Prayer

Our Father in heaven, hallowed be your name. Your kingdom come. Your will be done, on earth as it is in heaven. Thank you for my physical body. I confess I take it for granted. I assume so much of the brilliance you have built into my body. Open all of my perceptions to behold the miracle of your creation in me. And open my mind to understand my relationships with my brothers and sisters in Christ through the lens of my physical body. Come, Holy Spirit, reveal and teach to me the obvious profundities of these things. In Jesus' name, amen.

The Questions

- Today I want to ask you to observe the obvious: your body. Explore the interrelated movements so easily taken for granted. What do you notice? How does the human body reveal the practical and even mystical nature of human relationships in the body of Christ? What does this image of the human body reveal about who God is and what God is like?

Do People Actually Have Spiritual Gifts?

37

1 CORINTHIANS 12:27–31 | Now you are the body of Christ, and each one of you is a part of it. And God has placed in the church first of all apostles, second prophets, third teachers, then miracles, then gifts of healing, of helping, of guidance, and of different kinds of tongues. Are all apostles? Are all prophets? Are all teachers? Do all work miracles? Do all have gifts of healing? Do all speak in tongues? Do all interpret? Now eagerly desire the greater gifts.

Consider This

To those sanctified in Christ Jesus and called to be his holy people (i.e., us):

For several years now, I've wondered where we got the idea that we could give someone a multiple-choice inventory (test) to determine their spiritual gifts. Have you taken one of those tests before? They are sort of like a Meyers-Briggs personality test. Something tells me they weren't taking spiritual gifts tests in the first-century church. Something tells me this whole approach didn't even start until about 1981.

I don't mean to knock the test, and I certainly don't mean to shake anyone's confidence in their sense of giftings based on taking such tests. I just don't think it works this way. Spiritual gifts are supernatural. They don't necessarily match up with human giftedness or aptitudes or passions or things we like doing. It makes sense to us that it might work that way, but I'm just not sure this is what Scripture teaches on the subject.

Nor does it seem right that we would possess a spiritual gift in a kind of ownership way where it would be available on-demand. Here's my question: What if we don't actually have spiritual gifts, in the sense of possessing them? What if it's the other way around—spiritual gifts having or possessing us? New Testament Christianity points to our being filled with the person of the Holy Spirit.

I remember a conversation I had years ago with one of the great Methodist preachers of the last fifty years,

Dr. James Buskirk. We were talking about the gifts of the Holy Spirit. I may have misunderstood him, or I may be remembering him incorrectly—and I certainly don't want to misattribute something to him mistakenly. Here's what I remember him saying: "The Holy Spirit does not give gifts to you or to me for ministry. The Holy Spirit gives gifts in ministry." In other words, the Spirit gifts one person with the presence and power to minister to another person or persons according to their need in that moment. On one occasion the Spirit may give the gift of a miracle and on another occasion he may give the gift of prophecy.

It is my understanding and experience that the Holy Spirit works in power through all manner of gifts and manifestations where people are moving toward one another in love. Could it be that's why 1 Corinthians 13, the Love Manifesto, is tucked between chapters 12 and 14 on gifts and the body of Christ?

The Prayer

Our Father in heaven, hallowed be your name. Your kingdom come. Your will be done, on earth as it is in heaven. Thank you for the Holy Spirit and for the ways the Spirit gives gifts in ministry for the blessing of others and the building up of the body of Christ. Help me discern the gifts of the Spirit. Come, Holy Spirit, and give me the boldness to launch out into the work of God in ways of faith that count on the gifts being given to fulfill the calling and assignment. We pray in Jesus' name, amen.

The Questions
- What kind of love would you need to have for another person for you to move toward them in faith that the Holy Spirit would give a gift in the midst of your initiative to minister to them? How does this notion of the gifts of the Holy Spirit being given in ministry rather than being resident in a person on-demand resonate with you or not? How do you see the connection between the kind of love identified in the upcoming chapter 13 and the gifts of the Holy Spirit?

38 Why the Only Thing That Counts Is the Thing We Probably Aren't Counting

1 CORINTHIANS 13:1–13 | If I speak in the tongues of men or of angels, but do not have love, I am only a resounding gong or a clanging cymbal. If I have the gift of prophecy and can fathom all mysteries and all knowledge, and if I have a faith that can move mountains, but do not have love, I am nothing. If I give all I possess to the poor and give over my body to hardship that I may boast, but do not have love, I gain nothing.

Love is patient, love is kind. It does not envy, it does not boast, it is not proud. It does not dishonor others, it is not self-seeking, it is not easily angered, it keeps no record of wrongs. Love does not delight in evil but rejoices with the truth. It always protects, always trusts, always hopes, always perseveres.

Love never fails. But where there are prophecies, they will cease; where there are tongues, they will be stilled; where there is knowledge, it will pass away. For we know in part and we prophesy in part, but when completeness comes, what is in part disappears. When I was a child, I talked like a child, I thought like a child, I reasoned like a child. When I became a man, I put the ways of childhood behind me. For now we see only a reflection as in a mirror; then we shall see face to face. Now I know in part; then I shall know fully, even as I am fully known.

And now these three remain: faith, hope and love. But the greatest of these is love.

Consider This

To those sanctified in Christ Jesus and called to be his holy people (i.e., us):

We've heard it read a hundred times at weddings, which causes us (at least me) to associate this text with the warm, fuzzy, sentimental feelings that always ooze out of weddings. Said another way, this text—clearly one of the hardest texts in all of Scripture—comes off as soft and fluffy because of the context in which we have most often heard it.

Love, in the cultural, romance novel, bachelorette context is something completely different than love as defined in the Bible. It's fascinating to consider how the word "love" has become associated with the word "passion," particularly as relates to the way love gets commonly portrayed in the world (i.e., a passionate love affair). Passion becomes primarily associated with sexual expression. Here's the irony. The first definition for *passion* in many dictionaries is preceded by the words "archaic meaning" and followed by the word, "suffering." Passion means suffering. Passion actually means suffering love. Why else do we describe the crucifixion as the passion of Christ?

Love is not soft. Love is the most difficult thing in the world. Consider that the chapter uses the word "not" ten times, the word "always" four times, the word "no" once, and the word "love" eight times. These are the terms of definitive absolutes.

First Corinthians 13 must become for us an absolute manifesto. Somehow we need to keep this text before us every day. This is not pie-in-the-sky Hallmark card idealism. First Corinthians 13 is profound realism. As an exercise of faith and bold self-examination, I want to ask you to insert your name in every blank below. Read it aloud inserting your name in each blank.

_____ is patient, _____ is kind. _____ does not envy, _____ does not boast, _____ is not proud. _____ does not dishonor others, _____ is not self-seeking, _____ is not easily angered, _____ keeps no record of wrongs. _____ does not delight in evil but rejoices with the truth. _____ always protects, _____ always trusts, _____ always hopes, _____ always perseveres.

"This is impossible!" you say. And you are right, if it is solely up to you and me to become these things. Here's the big secret. Go back and insert the word "Jesus" in all the blanks. If these things are true about Jesus, and we know they are, and Jesus is in you, what does that say about you?

I'm going to start doing this little exercise of inserting my name in the blanks and reading this text aloud every day. We have a way of following our words. I see it as akin to prophesying over ourselves with the very Word of God. Will you join me in this? Let's just commit to the next seven days.

Why is this so urgently important? Because if we get everything else right and miss this, we have missed everything, but if we miss everything else and get this, we still have everything. Paul said to the Galatians, "The only thing that counts is faith expressing itself through love" (5:6b).

The Prayer

Our Father in heaven, hallowed be your name. Your kingdom come. Your will be done, on earth as it is in heaven. Thank you for challenging me with what is impossible for me. In this way, you lead me deeper into you, for whom nothing is impossible. You are my love, Jesus. Come, Holy Spirit, and so fill me with the love of Jesus that in encountering me they encounter him. Train me in this way of supernatural love. In Jesus' name, amen.

The Questions

- Is 1 Corinthians 13 an active possibility in your life or have you let it slip into unreachable idealism? Was it challenging to hear yourself reading your name in the exercise? What was that like for you? What will it take, or how can we get this vision of biblical love front and center in our everyday vision?

39 | Do You Eagerly Desire the Gifts of the Holy Spirit?

1 CORINTHIANS 14:1–5 | Follow the way of love and eagerly desire gifts of the Spirit, especially prophecy. For anyone who speaks in a tongue does not speak to people but to God. Indeed, no one understands them; they utter mysteries by the Spirit. But the one who prophesies speaks to people for their strengthening, encouraging and comfort. Anyone who speaks in a tongue edifies themselves, but the one who prophesies edifies the church. I would like every one of you to speak in tongues, but I would rather have you prophesy. The one who prophesies is greater than the one who speaks in tongues, unless someone interprets, so that the church may be edified.

Consider This

To those sanctified in Christ Jesus and called to be his holy people (i.e., us):

Okay, let's talk about tongues. It's been one of the controversies of the church from the start to the present day. On the one hand, the gift of tongues has been overemphasized as was the case with the Corinthians. On the other hand, the gift of tongues has been despised. Throughout history, branches of the church have insisted that speaking in tongues is the singular sign that one has been filled by the Holy Spirit, while other branches of the church have gone so far as to claim that speaking in tongues is a demonic expression.

So where's the truth in all this? Here's how I understand Paul on the subject. First, Paul clearly acknowledges tongues as a gift of the Holy Spirit. We need to understand Paul is responding to the problem that speaking in tongues had become in the Corinthian church. They were very much overemphasizing it. In chapter 12, Paul sets the gift of tongues in the larger context of the larger set of gifts of the Holy Spirit as well as in the larger context of the whole body of Christ. In chapter 13, Paul presents the overall governing dynamic with respect to the exercise of any gift of the Holy Spirit: love. Now that he has created this larger context, he moves into chapter 14, where he gets back to the specifics of the gift of tongues.

What does he say about tongues? Paul is all for tongues, but there is a governing rule over all the gifts. It is in the first part of verse 1.

Follow the way of love, . . .

Paul clearly defined what this means in the prior chapter. To this he adds,

eagerly desire gifts of the Spirit, . . .

This might be better translated to say, "Be longing for the utterances of the Spirit in your midst." Then he adds,

especially the gift of prophecy.

Love is the rule. If love is the rule, it means other people are the focus. If other people are the focus, then the gifts must be exercised in ways that benefit other people. Both gifts of tongues and prophecy are utterances that come directly from the Holy Spirit through the mouths of people. The difference? Tongues can only be understood by God and edify the one speaking in them (see v. 2). Prophecy can be understood by people and it edifies them (see v. 3). Paul says nothing negative about tongues, only that they are for private worship. (It's noted at the end of today's text in verse 5, that Paul would permit speaking in tongues in public worship if there is an interpretation. That's for another day.)

So what is the gift of prophecy we should especially desire? Verse 3 indicates prophecy means words given directly by the Spirit that "strengthen, encourage and comfort" other people. They are not words I have come up with, but direct words from the Holy Spirit given in the moment. Think of it as the difference between a download and a live stream. The typical sermon might be thought of more along the lines of a download. Someone has done research, developed creative thought, and prepared it for presentation to the church. Prophecy works like a live stream, coming spontaneously from the Holy Spirit through a person to another person or persons. Prophecy is not prepared or under the control of the one speaking.

Do you see the logic? Grow in the greatest gift of all, which is Holy Spirit–fueled love. Let this love move you toward others. Love others so deeply you eagerly desire to bless and help them beyond your own normal capacity to do so. Especially desire the Holy Spirit to work through you in ways that supernaturally strengthen, encourage, and comfort other people.

I don't know about you, but for most of my life I have, at best, attempted to "follow the way of love," but that's about it. I can't claim that I have "eagerly desired gifts from the Holy Spirit." I guess maybe I have eagerly desired them in the sense that I have eagerly desired to lose weight or get in shape. Nor can I say I have "especially" desired the gift of prophecy. It's been a gap or lapse in my own discipleship. I'm working on changing that. And you?

The Prayer

Our Father in heaven, hallowed be your name. Your kingdom come. Your will be done, on earth as it is in heaven. I am wondering, Lord, if my lack of eagerly desiring the gifts of the Spirit, especially the gift of prophecy, is a sign I am not walking in the way of love. For if I loved others as you love me, I would want to give them what only you can give them through me, which would come from your gifts. Come, Holy Spirit, and lead me in deep and real repentance on this point. I pray in Jesus' name, amen.

The Questions

- Are you staying with our 1 Corinthians 13 exercise? If not, do it now. Do you eagerly desire that the gifts of the Holy Spirit be expressed through you? What would it mean for that to happen in your life? What is the first step? What holds you back from especially desiring the gift of prophecy? Is it ignorance of the gift? Fear of being out of control? A lack of clarity of how it works? What is the first step in moving toward obeying this guidance from Scripture?

40 Why Worship Is Not about Preaching and Singing

1 CORINTHIANS 14:6–12 | Now, brothers and sisters, if I come to you and speak in tongues, what good will I be to you, unless I bring you some revelation or knowledge or prophecy or word of instruction? Even in the case of lifeless things that make sounds, such as the pipe or harp, how will anyone know what tune is being played unless there is a distinction in the notes? Again, if the trumpet does not sound a clear call, who will get ready for battle? So it is with you. Unless you speak intelligible words with your tongue, how will anyone know what you are saying? You will just be speaking into the air. Undoubtedly there are all sorts of languages in the world, yet none of them is without meaning. If then I do not grasp the meaning of what someone is saying, I am a foreigner to the speaker, and the speaker is a foreigner to me. So it is with you. Since you are eager for gifts of the Spirit, try to excel in those that build up the church.

Consider This

To those sanctified in Christ Jesus and called to be his holy people (i.e., us):

Why do we place such importance on gathering as a body and worshiping together? We could just worship at home, couldn't we? Why do we need to be together?

For most of my life, I have just accepted it as a non-negotiable commandment of God. You know, "the Bible says it—I believe it—that settles it," kind of thinking. I think I have mostly assumed God wants us there so we can worship him, but then I ask myself, "Does God really care about all this singing?" Then someone will say something like, "Worship is the central act of the people of God," as though that's supposed to clinch it. But it leaves me asking, "Why is worship the central act of the people of God?"

Paul continues in today's text with his argument about the gift and place of tongues in the gathered worship of the church. In the process he gives a key insight as to why gathered worship may be so essential.

So it is with you. Since you are eager for gifts of the Spirit, try to excel in those that build up the church.

We can be led in singing via pre-recorded worship or even through live streaming. We can listen to good preaching and from multiple preachers. We can even take the Lord's Supper in some semblance. The missing link, and one of the primary reasons for gathering in person for worship, is the exercise of the gifts of the Spirit in order to build up the body of Christ. Many are not missing this critical feature of worship in the absence of gathering, because it was not significantly present when they were able to gather.

Be reminded, Paul writes to the Corinthian church in order to speak into their particular problems. In the process we can glean some broad general principles about worship gatherings. First, worship is for God; therefore, worship must be clearly ordered by the Word of God. Second, worship is for the church; therefore, it must be spontaneously alive by the Spirit of God. Herein lives the rule of worship: Word and Spirit; divine order and divine spontaneity. And the rule of worship, it should be pointed out, is the rule of life. (Not "rules," mind you, but "rule.")

God, by his Word, orders the world into which God, by his Spirit, breathes life and love and creative power. You see, the church is the new world, the new creation of God's making. Worship, by Word and Spirit, by gathering and then scattering, is the way God does it.

The church has gone wrong when it has overemphasized one or another of these two prime elements: Word and Spirit. We have mistakenly thought the Word was about order and the Spirit about spontaneity. The truth is they are inseparably fused realities.

In another way, we have made the mistake of substituting sermon and music for Word and Spirit as though those were interchangeable terms. We have assumed worship was primarily about great preaching and great singing, hence we've brought worship down to the level of our own preferences. In the process we have often abandoned "the

Tradition," the living faith of the dead, while thinking we were getting rid of "traditionalism," the dead faith of the living.

Paul is not here talking about the order of worship. He speaks of order in worship. For Paul, order in worship means creating space for the work of Word and Spirit to create, strengthen, and build up the church. Worship is for the sake of the re-creative work of God in our midst so we might be the re-creative works of God in the midst of the broken world.

So what if we thought about our worship gatherings exclusively according to Word and Spirit? What would it mean to open ourselves up to the spontaneous work of the Holy Spirit in the midst of the Word-centered gathering of worship? It would mean more tongues confessing, "Jesus is Lord," on bended knees and more invitations of "Come, Holy Spirit" from surrendered hearts. It would mean eagerly desiring the gifts of the Spirit such that we might excel in building up the church.

So where do we begin?

The Prayer

Our Father in heaven, hallowed be your name. Your kingdom come. Your will be done, on earth as it is in heaven. Thank you for all the gifts of the Holy Spirit. Thank you even more for *the gift* of the Holy Spirit. Increase our under-standing of the gifts through expanding our practice of the gifts. We cannot be the church without the gifts of the Spirit. Come, Holy Spirit, and infuse us with more of you. We pray in Jesus' name, amen.

The Questions

- And so what of the confession, "Jesus is Lord"? Is it a daily confession that is meaning more and more every day? And what of the invitation "Come, Holy Spirit"? Is this becoming a more constant invitation in your daily life? Word and Spirit. These are the architects of the church. How are they becoming the architects of your own life and personal relationships? What will it take for you to "eagerly desire the gifts of the Holy Spirit" and especially those that build up the church?

41 Why Greeting Your Seatmates in Church Won't Cut It Anymore

1 CORINTHIANS 14:13–19 | For this reason the one who speaks in a tongue should pray that they may interpret what they say. For if I pray in a tongue, my spirit prays, but my mind is unfruitful. So what shall I do? I will pray with my spirit, but I will also pray with my understanding; I will sing with my spirit, but I will also sing with my understanding. Otherwise when you are praising God in the Spirit, how can someone else, who is now put in the position of an inquirer, say "Amen" to your thanksgiving, since they do not know what you are saying? You are giving thanks well enough, but no one else is edified.

I thank God that I speak in tongues more than all of you. But in the church I would rather speak five intelligible words to instruct others than ten thousand words in a tongue.

Consider This

To those sanctified in Christ Jesus and called to be his holy people (i.e., us):

Many people are against the gift of tongues because they do not understand it. Others are opposed to the gift because they do not have it, and they have been made to feel somehow diminished as a Christian as a result. If anybody thought Paul had a problem with the gift of tongues, he just blew that theory out of the water.

I thank God that I speak in tongues more than all of you.

The governing question with respect to the exercise of the gifts of the Holy Spirit is whether it builds up the church. A gift from the Holy Spirit is an exceedingly good thing; however, if exercised to the detriment of other people it can be a bad thing. It comes down to loving other people. Paul brought his point to crystal clarity when he said in the prior chapter, "If I speak in the tongues of men or of angels, but have not love, I am only a resounding gong or a clanging cymbal" (1 Cor. 13:1).

When is the last time you were standing near a pair of cymbals being relentlessly banged together? Get in touch with that experience and you have the approximate value of speaking in tongues in the midst of public worship where what you are saying cannot be understood by others.

In the public worship of the church, the primary concern is whether those gathered can understand what is being said. Again, Paul is crystal clear:

But in the church I would rather speak five intelligible words to instruct others than ten thousand words in a tongue.

I wonder if there is an even more expanded application of this principle in our worship gatherings. I'll be honest, for most of my going to church life, the focus has pretty much been on what's happening up front. Sure, there was always the "Passing of the Peace," which pretty much got reduced to a "greet your neighbor" time (who you already greeted at Sunday school), but we weren't too much even aware of each other in your typical worship service down at Dumas First United Methodist Church.

What if our worship gatherings became as much about each other as they were about God? Something in us resists that notion as it offends our sense of what worship is. Here's my question: Why wouldn't God want us to be about each other when we are gathered together to worship him? Reasoning a bit from below, imagine a group of a dozen siblings all coming home to visit their mother and father, yet all the conversation and interaction only happens between the siblings and the parents. Imagine how the parents would feel with their kids politely ignoring each other. It's like they weren't even there together. Or imagine a Division 1 football game between the top-rated teams in the country and the fans were all focused on the field with no interaction among each other. That gets close to many worship gatherings we see today.

Worship is a golden opportunity for the expression of the love of God. On that we all agree. But isn't worship also a golden opportunity for the expression of the love of one another? The last time I checked, the most significant experience Jesus wants not-yet-believers to have with the church is that of exclaiming, "My how they love one another." Imagine how it would bless the heart of God to see gatherings of worship where his people were irresistibly drawn into blessing one another in all kinds of ways.

What would need to change in our weekly gatherings for this to be realized?

The Prayer

Our Father in heaven, hallowed be your name. Your kingdom come. Your will be done, on earth as it is in heaven. Prepare us to come together with a deep and renewed love for you and for one another. Let our worship gatherings become places of concentrated love, love that combusts into power that lead to impossible things becoming possible. In Jesus' name, amen.

The Questions

- Can you remember being part of a worship service where you experienced the palpable love of God being expressed between the people? What was that like? Have you been in worship services where you felt like you were alone in the midst of a crowd of people? What was that like? What might it mean for you to move toward others with the love of God (beyond polite greetings) in the worship gatherings held in your community? What holds you back?

42 The Big Reason God Writes Us Letters

1 CORINTHIANS 14:20–25 | Brothers and sisters, stop thinking like children. In regard to evil be infants, but in your thinking be adults. In the Law it is written:

> "With other tongues
>   and through the lips of foreigners
> I will speak to this people,
>   but even then they will not listen to me,
> says the Lord."

Tongues, then, are a sign, not for believers but for unbelievers; prophecy, however, is not for unbelievers but for believers. So if the whole church comes together and everyone speaks in tongues, and inquirers or unbelievers come in, will they not say that you are out of your mind? But if an unbeliever or an inquirer comes in while everyone is prophesying, they are convicted of sin and are brought under judgment by all, as the secrets of their hearts are laid bare. So they will fall down and worship God, exclaiming, "God is really among you!"

Consider This

To those sanctified in Christ Jesus and called to be his holy people (i.e., us):

As we come closer to the home stretch for Paul's first letter to the Corinthian church, I find myself trying to get a big picture view of the whole letter once again. For most of my Bible reading life this never occurred to me—that I needed to grasp the big picture before I could really understand the small one.

The last five words in today's text gives us a profound sense of the big picture in Paul's letter to the Corinthians.

So they will fall down and worship God, exclaiming, "God is really among you!"

Paul's overarching intent of this whole letter, if not all of his letters, is that the people of God would evoke this kind of response from the not-yet-believing world. "God is really among you!" All of Paul's counsel and correction aim to bring people into the only outfit on the face of the planet created and sustained by the Holy Spirit: the church. The purpose of the church is to manifest the palpable reality of the embodied presence of God on earth and this for the sake of blessing all of creation. The power by which this happens is the love of God, which we know because of Jesus Christ. When the love of God is unleashed in the relationships among the followers of Jesus, people will find themselves exclaiming, "God is really among you!"

We always think about 1 Corinthians 13 as some kind of abstract poem when in reality it was very particularly addressed to the problems in the Corinthians church. Try this inverse, antithetical interpretation of the text to get at what Paul was addressing.

Sin is impatient, sin is unkind. Sin envies, boasts, and is filled with pride. Sin dishonors others, is self-seeking, is easily angered and keeps records of wrongs. Sin delights in evil and rejoices in lies. Sin never protects, never trusts, never hopes, never perseveres. Sin always fails.

The opposite of love is not hate. It is sin. And the definition of sin is, "missing the mark of love." It is the pervasiveness of sin in our relationships that effectively says to others, "God is not really among us!"

Paul's effort is not to bridle sin. It is to unleash love. Go back through the letter and see if this is not the case. All this stuff about not eating food sacrificed to idols and sexual immorality and marriage and singleness and gifts and the body and so on—it's all about shepherding a group of people to live together in the power of the Holy Spirit to the end that the world will exclaim, "God is really among you!"

The Prayer

Our Father in heaven, hallowed be your name. Your kingdom come. Your will be done, on earth as it is in heaven. Let it be said of our lives, our families, our churches, and even our cities, "God is really among you!" We know it will not be said until it is experienced as real. So make the love of God in Jesus Christ to be the palpable reality of our existence. Come, Holy Spirit, and train me to repent in all the ways I must, to turn from sin and be infused with your love. I pray in Jesus' name, amen.

The Questions

- Do you find yourself managing sin or eradicating it in your life? Evaluate this claim: the strength of your relationship with God will never exceed the love in your relationships with others. True or false? Why? "God is really among you!" Would that be the exclamation of people looking in on your church? Your family?

Why New Testament Worship Is More like a Potluck than a Production

43

1 CORINTHIANS 14:26–33 | What then shall we say, brothers and sisters? When you come together, each of you has a hymn, or a word of instruction, a revelation, a tongue or an interpretation. Everything must be done so that the church may be built up. If anyone speaks in a tongue, two—or at the most three—should speak, one at a time, and someone must interpret. If there is no interpreter, the speaker should keep quiet in the church and speak to himself and to God.

Two or three prophets should speak, and the others should weigh carefully what is said. And if a revelation comes to someone who is sitting down, the first speaker should stop. For you can all prophesy in turn so that everyone may be instructed and encouraged. The spirits of prophets are subject to the control of prophets. For God is not a God of disorder but of peace—as in all the congregations of the Lord's people.

Consider This

To those sanctified in Christ Jesus and called to be his holy people (i.e., us):

Who knew? Worship is a potluck, and everybody brings a dish. Picking up an earlier analogy, worship is a team sport, and everybody plays.

When you come together, each of you has a hymn, or a word of instruction, a revelation, a tongue or an interpretation.

Somewhere along the way the situation got flipped. These days it's more like, "When you come together, each of you take a seat and focus your attention on the gifted leaders who are up front leading the worship service."

What happened? Somehow, somewhere along the way, worship became more of a production than a potluck. As I previously said, we now have the strange situation where the coaches take the field and the players sit in the stands. And it is completely normal to us. It seems a long way from the New Testament vision of Christian worship. I'm not saying what we are doing is not Christian. It's just that it doesn't seem to be very New Testament.

Here's where this has led us. The primary reason most people go to church is in order to consume. It's the same kind of mentality we bring to a restaurant. As a consequence, we evaluate and critique and assess the food and the service. And I don't mean to say church is not a place to receive from God. Paul makes clear the primary reason for joining together with others for worship. It is as follows:

Everything must be done so that the church may be built up.

We go to church to give, to make an offering of ourselves as a living sacrifice, to build up the body of Christ. Church is not about showing up for a worship service, but showing up to serve God and one another as an act of corporate worship.

I love this notion of doing church. Someone brings a word from Scripture the Lord has impressed on them. Another offers a word of encouragement. Yet another brings a hymn or a psalm or a spiritual song. Someone else speaks in an unknown tongue, and it is interpreted. This is New Testament church. It's orderly and beautiful and powerful. This looks like the body doing its work to build itself up in the strength of the Holy Spirit.

The Prayer

Our Father in heaven, hallowed be your name. Your kingdom come. Your will be done, on earth as it is in heaven. Thank you for the way you gift the body of Christ through all of its members. Would you lead our local churches to be places where the people come not to consume a presentation but to converge as the body, everyone playing their part? Come, Holy Spirit, and lead us into the kingdom vision for the gathered people of God.

We pray in Jesus' name, amen.

The Questions

- So before we get down on what we are presently doing on Sundays in worship (which is often very faithful and good), how about we try taking this approach from today's text in a small group of friends? What if you knew the gathered church was counting on you to bring a gift for worship with you? How would that change the way you thought about going to church? What would it mean for you to begin asking God to give you gifts for the sake of building up the body of Christ? We don't have to whole-sale change our present Sunday worship approach (which seems impossible) to bring gifts with us to the gathering that we might be prepared to quietly offer, perhaps to a friend or even a stranger sitting down the row, as the Spirit prompts us.

The Definitive Guide to the Gifts of the Holy Spirit

1 CORINTHIANS 14:34–40 | Women should remain silent in the churches. They are not allowed to speak, but must be in submission, as the law says. If they want to inquire about something, they should ask their own husbands at home; for it is disgraceful for a woman to speak in the church.

Or did the word of God originate with you? Or are you the only people it has reached? If anyone thinks they are a prophet or otherwise gifted by the Spirit, let them acknowledge that what I am writing to you is the Lord's command. But if anyone ignores this, they will themselves be ignored.

Therefore, my brothers and sisters, be eager to prophesy, and do not forbid speaking in tongues. But everything should be done in a fitting and orderly way.

Consider This

To those sanctified in Christ Jesus and called to be his holy people (i.e., us):

And so, we come to the close of our conversation about the gifts of the Holy Spirit, yet there's so much more to learn. Remember how we began?

Walk in the way of love and eagerly desire spiritual gifts, especially the gift of prophecy.

Paul closes the chapter in similar fashion as he began it:

Therefore, my brothers and sisters, be eager to prophesy, and do not forbid speaking in tongues.

There is no definitive treatment of the gifts in Scripture. Paul engages them here in 1 Corinthians and also in Romans 12. So where are we to learn more? Should we read more books about them? While that's not a bad idea, I think this is an area where we will learn more from experience than from reading.

Walk in the way of love. The gifts of God flow from the love of God. What if the gifts are only entrusted to those who are walking in the way of love?

Eagerly desire spiritual gifts. Why? We desperately want the gifts so we can be empowered to love other people better. There's another possible reason—so we might accrue more power for ourselves. If we eagerly desire the love of God, we will have the power of God. The corollary is not equally true though. If we eagerly desire the power of God, it does not follow that we will possess the love of God.

I think the most critical teaching in the whole chapter has to do with the sequence. First, walk in the way of love. Second, eagerly desire spiritual gifts. The more we love one another the more we want to help one another.

It brings to mind the singular command of Jesus. Love one another as I have loved you. You know where I think we can find a definitive biblical treatment on the gifts of the Spirit? It has only just now occurred to me. The life of Jesus. Yes, it seems obvious now, but doesn't that make sense? Could it be possible that we can see all the gifts of the Holy Spirit operative in Jesus' life at one point or another in the Gospels? His exercise of the gifts are pure expressions of love for people.

The Prayer

Our Father in heaven, hallowed be your name. Your kingdom come. Your will be done, on earth as it is in heaven. Thank you for all the gifts of the Holy Spirit. Thank you even more for *the gift* of the Holy Spirit. Come, Holy Spirit, and fill us with the life of Jesus that we might walk in the way of love, eagerly desire your gifts, and so build up the body of Christ. We pray in Jesus' name, amen.

The Questions

- Are you getting the sequence right? Step 1: Walk in the way of love. Step 2: Eagerly desire spiritual gifts. Does this sequence make sense to you? What gifts of the Holy

Spirit do you eagerly desire in order to be of help to other people? What stories and scenes come to mind in the life of Jesus where you can see gifts of the Spirit at work? What do you learn about the gifts from examining these stories?

Note: I would be remiss not to at least reference the controversial subject in today's text admonishing women to keep silent in the church. This is a complex text whose context reveals a much deeper understanding of what Paul was actually addressing here. Try an Internet search for "Seedbed women in ministry" to get our full take on this text.

Where Does the Gospel Begin? It Matters What You Think

45

1 CORINTHIANS 15:1–11 | Now, brothers and sisters, I want to remind you of the gospel I preached to you, which you received and on which you have taken your stand. By this gospel you are saved, if you hold firmly to the word I preached to you. Otherwise, you have believed in vain.

For what I received I passed on to you as of first importance: that Christ died for our sins according to the Scriptures, that he was buried, that he was raised on the third day according to the Scriptures, and that he appeared to Cephas, and then to the Twelve. After that, he appeared to more than five hundred of the brothers and sisters at the same time, most of whom are still living, though some have fallen asleep. Then he appeared to James, then to all the apostles, and last of all he appeared to me also, as to one abnormally born.

For I am the least of the apostles and do not even deserve to be called an apostle, because I persecuted the church of God. But by the grace of God I am what I am, and his grace to me was not without effect. No, I worked harder than all of them— yet not I, but the grace of God that was with me. Whether, then, it is I or they, this is what we preach, and this is what you believed.

Consider This

To those sanctified in Christ Jesus and called to be his holy people (i.e., us):

What is the gospel? If someone asked you to answer the question, how would you do it?

Perhaps the bigger question is, where do you start? Does the gospel begin with a problem? Must you have bad news in order to have good news? Is the gospel a bad news/good news scenario? The short answer: no.

The gospel does not begin with sin. The gospel begins with God's good creation. The gospel begins with a world where the crowning creation are the image-bearers of God. We talk so much about original sin, when we need to remember what preceded sin—original goodness and glory. The good news is God created a world filled with righteousness, peace, and joy in the Holy Spirit.

Okay, I think I made a mistake. I could go back and erase the prior material, but I will leave it in order to demonstrate the kind of thinking I'm trying to correct. The first mistake is to think the gospel begins with the problem—sin. The second mistake is to think the gospel begins with creation—culminating with the creation of people.

The gospel begins much earlier than sin or creation or people. How about an obvious insight? The gospel begins with God. The good news is before anything else, there was God. Putting it that way is not enough though. Who is God? What is God like? Is this God like Allah? The gospel begins with God, who is Father, Son, and Holy Spirit, a triune community of holy love, who existed before time and exists beyond time and who will exist eternally after time ends. The gospel begins with perfect love in the perfect union of a God who is three in one. This is very, very good news.

At the core of all eternity dwells the triune God of perfect unity in a community of holy, creative love. From this eternal community comes a creation of extravagant diversity. Only after all of this unprecedented, unequaled glory and goodness do we get the bad news of sin and death. Sin and death and evil are a major problem for the world and the human race, but not for God. That's good news. Because the gospel does not begin with sin it will not let sin prevail. The overwhelming love of God overcomes sin in a way only divine love could do.

For what I received I passed on to you as of first importance: that Christ died for our sins according to the Scriptures, that he was buried, that he was raised on the third day according to the Scriptures.

Where does the gospel begin? It matters what you think.

The Prayer

Our Father in heaven, hallowed be your name. Your kingdom come. Your will be done, on earth as it is in heaven. The gospel begins with you. In fact, Lord Jesus, you are the gospel. Come, Holy Spirit, and enlarge our vision of this good news. We need a fuller picture. Teach us to begin even before the beginning, with your preexistent goodness and glory. We pray in Jesus' name, amen.

The Questions

• What are the implications of beginning the gospel with sin? With creation? With God: Father, Son, and Holy Spirit? If the magnitude of God's goodness is incomparably greater than the magnitude of sin, why do we struggle so with sin? What will it take for the gospel to take on greater power in our own lives?

46 What If They Found the Bones of Jesus?

1 CORINTHIANS 15:12–28 | But if it is preached that Christ has been raised from the dead, how can some of you say that there is no resurrection of the dead? If there is no resurrection of the dead, then not even Christ has been raised. And if Christ has not been raised, our preaching is useless and so is your faith. More than that, we are then found to be false witnesses about God, for we have testified about God that he raised Christ from the dead. But he did not raise him if in fact the dead are not raised. For if the dead are not raised, then Christ has not been raised either. And if Christ has not been raised, your faith is futile; you are still in your sins. Then those also who have fallen asleep in Christ are lost. If only for this life we have hope in Christ, we are of all people most to be pitied.

But Christ has indeed been raised from the dead, the firstfruits of those who have fallen asleep. For since death came through a man, the resurrection of the dead comes also through a man. For as in Adam all die, so in Christ all will be made alive. But each in turn: Christ, the firstfruits; then, when he comes, those who belong to him. Then the end will come, when he hands over the kingdom to God the Father after he has destroyed all dominion, authority and power. For he must reign until he has put all his enemies under his feet. The last enemy to be destroyed is death. For he "has put everything under his feet." Now when it says that "everything" has been put under him, it is clear that this does not include God himself, who put everything under Christ. When he has done this, then the Son himself will be made subject to him who put everything under him, so that God may be all in all.

Consider This

To those sanctified in Christ Jesus and called to be his holy people (i.e., us):

It was my first class in my first year of seminary: "The Philosophy of Christian Religion." Dr. Jerry Walls was the professor and one of my favorites. I will forever remember the jarring question he posed to the class on that first day. It went like this: If today you received news of incontrovertible evidence that the bones of Jesus had been discovered, would you still retain your Christian faith?

He asked for a show of hands of those who would still believe, and practically every hand in the class shot up. People had obviously not accepted the hypothesis. He emphasized that we had to accept the hypothetical fact that the bones of Jesus had been discovered in order to respond to the question. Provided the verifiable truth of the claim that the bones of Jesus had been found, would you still have faith in Jesus Christ? Still all hands rose with certainty into the air. He asked a third time and to strengthen the hypothetical, he added that the likes of Billy Graham had verified the news. This time only one person lowered their hand. Dr. Walls championed this lone dissenter, looked at the rest of the class, and exclaimed, "With the exception of this one student, all of you are liberals." (By this he meant that matters of faith are governed primarily by human experience rather than historical verities.)

As one of the students whose hand was raised high, I was stunned and yet quickly realized he was exactly right.

And if Christ has not been raised, your faith is futile; you are still in your sins.

If our faith is not anchored in the historical bodily resurrection of Jesus of Nazareth then we, as Paul put it, "are of all people most to be pitied."

It brings the old hymn to mind, "You ask me how I know he lives. He lives within my heart." No. We might more properly say, "You ask me how I know he lives. On the third day he arose from the dead!" Our faith, while decidedly experiential, is not built on our experience but on the bedrock, foundational fact of the historical bodily resurrection of Jesus, as they say, period.

In today's text, Paul comes at it from the other side. The Corinthians weren't exactly denying the bodily resurrection of Jesus. They were denying their own bodily resurrection. Paul told them that to deny the resurrection of the body was also to deny the resurrection of Jesus. In other words, the bodily resurrection of Jesus was the beginning of the end of death: "the firstfruits of those who have fallen asleep." Because Christ is raised from the dead, all those who are in Christ will also be raised from the dead. There is no such thing as one without the other.

The resurrection of Jesus Christ is not a spiritual metaphor. Nor is it a mythical reality. While there is a substantial body of evidence that may be marshaled in support of the resurrection, it cannot ultimately be proven. It is a matter of faith. One either believes in the efficacious, historical, bodily resurrection of Jesus . . . or one does not. The former is a Christian. The latter is something else entirely.

The Prayer

Our Father in heaven, hallowed be your name. Your kingdom come. Your will be done, on earth as it is in heaven. Sort out our faith for us. Clarify it so that our faith is anchored in the historical event of the resurrection of Jesus and not merely our experience. Come, Holy Spirit, and anchor our faith in the bedrock event and reality of the resurrection—nothing more or less. We pray in Jesus' name, amen.

The Questions

• Do you believe in the historical, bodily resurrection of Jesus Christ? On what do you base this belief? Why would you say we are of all people "most to be pitied," if the resurrection of Jesus Christ is not ultimately true? So what if they found the bones of Jesus today? Would you still be a Christian? Why or why not?

How the Christian Faith Becomes Something Other than the Christian Faith

1 CORINTHIANS 15:29–41 | Now if there is no resurrection, what will those do who are baptized for the dead? If the dead are not raised at all, why are people baptized for them? And as for us, why do we endanger ourselves every hour? I face death every day—yes, just as surely as I boast about you in Christ Jesus our Lord. If I fought wild beasts in Ephesus with no more than human hopes, what have I gained? If the dead are not raised,

> "Let us eat and drink,
>   for tomorrow we die."

Do not be misled: "Bad company corrupts good character." Come back to your senses as you ought, and stop sinning; for there are some who are ignorant of God—I say this to your shame.

But someone will ask, "How are the dead raised? With what kind of body will they come?" How foolish! What you sow does not come to life unless it dies. When you sow, you do not plant the body that will be, but just a seed, perhaps of wheat or of something else. But God gives it a body as he has determined, and to each kind of seed he gives its own body. Not all flesh is the same: People have one kind of flesh, animals have another, birds another and fish another. There are also heavenly bodies and there are earthly bodies; but the splendor of the heavenly bodies is one kind, and the splendor of the earthly bodies is another. The sun has one kind of splendor, the moon another and the stars another; and star differs from star in splendor.

Consider This

To those sanctified in Christ Jesus and called to be his holy people (i.e., us):

Yesterday we closed with the assertion that in order to be a Christian—in the sense that the church has taught and affirmed from its inception—you had to believe in the bodily resurrection of Jesus Christ. The Christian faith means nothing apart from the historical event of the bodily resurrection of Jesus Christ.

The death and resurrection of Jesus Christ has been interpreted to mean many things through the centuries when in reality it means only two things: the defeat of sin and the end of death. This alone is what motivated the apostle Paul to say things like this:

I face death every day—yes, just as surely as I boast about you in Christ Jesus our Lord. If I fought wild beasts in Ephesus with no more than human hopes, what have I gained? If the dead are not raised, "Let us eat and drink, for tomorrow we die."

The Christian faith has nothing to do with growing more prosperous, though it has led to the prospering of many. It is not a self-improvement strategy, though it has improved the lives of countless millions. The Christian faith is not a new idealism for a utopian society, though it holds the capacity to give rise to the kingdom of heaven on earth. It is not an ideology for social reformation, though it has probably given birth to more social reform than all the other religions combined in the history of the world.

We get into trouble and drift from our faith when we make it about its effects more than its core agenda. In other words, the Christian faith—also known as the life, death, and resurrection of Jesus Christ—is about the defeat of sin and the end of death. The defeat of sin and the end of death leads to all manner of human flourishing and prospering. It leads to the improvement of human beings beyond measure. It gives birth to endless creative reform and innovation in every sector of society, favoring the lifting up of the poor and the inclusion of the outcast. It gives rise to nothing short of the establishment of the kingdom of God, on earth as it is in heaven.

It sounds like an obvious idea, but this is the way the Christian faith becomes something other than the Christian faith. No matter what it is that we are doing and how much good it contributes to others, if it is not directly connected with the defeat of sin and the end of death, we might as well be the Kiwanis Club. Taking it a step further, if what we are calling the Christian faith is not solely dependent on the life, death, and resurrection of Jesus Christ, it is not the Christian faith.

The Corinthians were quickly turning the Christian faith into something other than the Christian faith. It had Christian forms and practices but it was drifting from the core story and truth of the gospel. This drift was ground zero of the Corinthian chaos. It's why Paul would know nothing save Christ crucified and risen from the dead among them.

If the church could be replaced by the Rotary Club (no offense intended to the Rotary Club), the church is simply something other than the church. Paul didn't face death every day, fight wild beasts, rot in prison cells, and the like for our bake sales.

The Prayer

Our Father in heaven, hallowed be your name. Your kingdom come. Your will be done, on earth as it is in heaven. Thank you for the simplicity of the gospel. Forgive us for the ways we make it complicated and miss the point. Come, Holy Spirit, and reveal the simple gospel that we might know its comprehensive impacts. We pray in Jesus' name, amen.

The Questions

- Do you get what I'm saying about disconnecting the gospel's outcomes from its core truth? Have you ever been part of churches that do good without doing the gospel? What distinguishes your local church from a social organization or a charity? How do you connect your own efforts in mission and ministry to the core agenda of the defeat of sin and the end of death?

48 The Difference between the Story and the Plot

1 CORINTHIANS 15:42–58 | So will it be with the resurrection of the dead. The body that is sown is perishable, it is raised imperishable; it is sown in dishonor, it is raised in glory; it is sown in weakness, it is raised in power; it is sown a natural body, it is raised a spiritual body.

If there is a natural body, there is also a spiritual body. So it is written: "The first man Adam became a living being"; the last Adam, a life-giving spirit. The spiritual did not come first, but the natural, and after that the spiritual. The first man was of the dust of the earth; the second man is of heaven. As was the earthly man, so are those who are of the earth; and as is the heavenly man, so also are those who are of heaven. And just as we have borne the image of the earthly man, so shall we bear the image of the heavenly man.

I declare to you, brothers and sisters, that flesh and blood cannot inherit the kingdom of God, nor does the perishable inherit the imperishable. Listen, I tell you a mystery: We will not all sleep, but we will all be changed—in a flash, in the twinkling of an eye, at the last trumpet. For the trumpet will sound, the dead will be raised imperishable, and we will be changed. For the perishable must clothe itself with the imper- ishable, and the mortal with immortality. When the perishable has been clothed with the imperishable, and the mortal with immortality, then the saying that is written will come true: "Death has been swallowed up in victory."

"Where, O death, is your victory?

Where, O death, is your sting?" The sting of death is sin, and the power of sin is the law. But thanks be to God! He gives us the victory through our Lord Jesus Christ.

Therefore, my dear brothers and sisters, stand firm. Let nothing move you. Always give yourselves fully to the work of the Lord, because you know that your labor in the Lord is not in vain.

Consider This

To those sanctified in Christ Jesus and called to be his holy people (i.e., us):

The Bible has little to nothing to say about heaven. It says quite a lot about the resurrection of the dead. To be clear, this is not to diminish the reality of heaven. It is time we brought more attention to the final outcome and ultimate state of affairs—the resurrection of the dead.

According to the Bible, the ultimate state of affairs is not a communion of disembodied souls removed from the earth. Far from it; the Bible begins with creation and ends with new creation. The story is not sin and salvation. That is the glorious plot line. The story is creation to new creation. The story is not burial and heaven. It is death and resurrection. The great creed of the apostles tells us Jesus ascended into heaven and that he will return to judge the quick and the dead. Notice how the creed closes. I believe in . . . the resurrection of the body and the life everlasting.

Now, before you start throwing things at me, let's be clear about something. Heaven is real. "For we know that if the earthly tent we live in is destroyed, we have a building from God, an eternal house in heaven, not built by human hands" (2 Cor. 5:1). The Bible clearly says to be absent from the body is to be present to the Lord (see 2 Corinthians 5:8). Paul said to live is Christ and to die is gain (see Philippians 1:21). Heaven is real—just not ultimate. Today's text (indeed the whole of the fifteenth chapter) reveals the ultimate reality.

So will it be with the resurrection of the dead. The body that is sown is perishable, it is raised imperishable; it is sown in dishonor, it is raised in glory; it is sown in weakness, it is raised in power; it is sown a natural body, it is raised a spiritual body.

Every Easter I do my best to take my children to my hometown to be with my parents and extended family. Without fail, on Holy Saturday, we gather ourselves into a caravan of vehicles and make pilgrimage to the Walnut Lake Cemetery in Pickens, Arkansas. Upon arrival, we walk together to the family burial plot. We share stories about Meemaw and Peepaw who have preceded us in death, we talk about Jesus and the gospel, and then we recite the Apostles' Creed together. After that we do a curious thing. We fan out through the cemetery, walking among the tombstones, declaring the resurrection of Jesus. Admittedly, as the cousins get older it gets harder to persuade their full-throated participation in this closing act of Holy Saturday. Forever ringing in my ears and in my soul are their childlike voices shouting at the top of their lungs—to the hundreds upon hundreds of granite monuments, each marking the resting place—not of a soul but a body: "Jesus Christ is risen from the dead!"

I like to think of these dearly departed saints, seated in the great cloud of witnesses, looking over the balcony of heaven and smiling, elbowing one another in anticipation and maybe slapping high-fives as these eternal words ring out in resounding victory.

When the perishable has been clothed with the imperishable, and the mortal with immortality, then the saying that is written will come true: "Death has been swallowed up in victory. Where, O death, is your victory? Where, O death, is your sting?"

The Prayer

Our Father in heaven, hallowed be your name. Your kingdom come. Your will be done, on earth as it is in heaven. I believe in the resurrection of the body and the life everlasting. Thank you, Jesus, for the resurrection of the body and all this means, now and forever. Thank you for this body of mine, perishable as it is, and that you will one day clothe it with an imperishable body. Come, Holy Spirit, and fill our imaginations with these eternal yet earthly verities. Stretch our perception beyond our comprehension and grant us awe at what we can grasp and joy in all the vast glory that remains beyond our reach. Until that day, we pray in Jesus' name, amen.

The Questions

- Are you growing in your understanding of the difference and relationship between the plot of sin and salvation, death and heaven, and the grand story of creation to new creation and the resurrection of the body and the life everlasting? How does it challenge and enrich your faith and life?

And Now for Something Completely Different . . .

49

1 CORINTHIANS 16:1–24 | Now about the collection for the Lord's people: Do what I told the Galatian churches to do. On the first day of every week, each one of you should set aside a sum of money in keeping with your income, saving it up, so that when I come no collections will have to be made. Then, when I arrive, I will give letters of introduction to the men you approve and send them with your gift to Jerusalem. If it seems advisable for me to go also, they will accompany me.

After I go through Macedonia, I will come to you—for I will be going through Macedonia. Perhaps I will stay with you for a while, or even spend the winter, so that you can help me on my journey, wherever I go. For I do not want to see you now and make only a passing visit; I hope to spend some time with you, if the Lord permits. But I will stay on at Ephesus until Pentecost, because a great door for effective work has opened to me, and there are many who oppose me.

When Timothy comes, see to it that he has nothing to fear while he is with you, for he is carrying on the work of the Lord, just as I am. No one, then, should treat him with contempt. Send him on his way in peace so that he may return to me. I am expecting him along with the brothers.

Now about our brother Apollos: I strongly urged him to go to you with the brothers. He was quite unwilling to go now, but he will go when he has the opportunity.

Be on your guard; stand firm in the faith; be courageous; be strong. Do everything in love.

You know that the household of Stephanas were the first converts in Achaia, and they have devoted themselves to the service of the Lord's people. I urge you, brothers and sisters, to submit to such people and to everyone who joins in the work and labors at it. I was glad when Stephanas, Fortunatus and Achaicus arrived, because they have supplied what was lacking from you. For they refreshed my spirit and yours also. Such men deserve recognition.

The churches in the province of Asia send you greetings. Aquila and Priscilla greet you warmly in the Lord, and so does the church that meets at their house. All the brothers and sisters here send you greetings. Greet one another with a holy kiss.

I, Paul, write this greeting in my own hand.

If anyone does not love the Lord, let that person be cursed! Come, Lord!

The grace of the Lord Jesus be with you.

My love to all of you in Christ Jesus. Amen.

Consider This

Where do we go from the fifteenth chapter of Paul's first letter to the Corinthians? We can practically hear the blast of the last trumpet as we imagine the imperishable resurrection bodies with which we will be clothed at the great resurrection of the dead. Paul has just taken the gospel from the grave to stratospheric celestial heights and where does he go next?

Yep . . . the announcements. The guy starts reading the announcements.

Now about the collection for the Lord's people:

After I go through Macedonia,

When Timothy comes,

Now about our brother Apollos:

True confession—when I wrote the original Daily Text entries for this series online, I stopped at the end of chapter 15. I couldn't bring myself to write about the announcements for some reason. I wanted to put an exclamation on resurrection and move on. And that's my problem. Somehow, I fail to realize that the announcements are as inspired by the Holy Spirit as the rest of the letter.

Isn't that true of our lives? We fail to realize unless the gospel of Jesus works itself out in the nitty-gritty level of our everyday, ordinary lives, it never leaves the pages of our Bibles. It's housekeeping. That's exactly what it is: housekeeping. Housekeeping is always the very next step of the gospel of Jesus. It goes to housekeeping, or it goes nowhere.

Go back now and read through 1 Corinthians 16, because chances are (if you are anything like me) you lightly skimmed it if you read it at all. Read it with care, and after that, it's time to get back to the announcement-level work of your own life—the to-do lists, the calendar, the budget, the everyday housekeeping stuff of it all. That's where the gospel must land—the sanctified stuff of housekeeping.

It is fitting for us to end with the word with which we have begun every single one of these daily entries. Perhaps you thought I forgot it this time.

To those sanctified in Christ Jesus and called to be his holy people (i.e., us):

The grace of the Lord Jesus be with you.
My love to all of you in Christ Jesus. Amen.

The Prayer

Our Father in heaven, hallowed be your name. Your kingdom come. Your will be done, on earth as it is in heaven. Thank you for the foolishness of the cross, the power of the resurrection, and, yes, for the announcements. Come, Holy Spirit, and weave all of this together in my heart, my home, my church, and my city into the messy seamlessness of a beautiful whole. Lead me now into the glorious and holy work of housekeeping—in Jesus' name, amen.

The Questions

- From the resurrection of the body and the life everlasting to the announcements. How will the deepest truth of the gospel reach the most ordinary and mundane levels of your everyday life? Are you seeing the connections?

THE SOWER'S CREED

Today,
I sow for a great awakening.

Today,
I stake everything on the promise of the Word of God.
I depend entirely on the power of the Holy Spirit.
I have the same mind in me that was in Christ Jesus.
Because Jesus is good news and Jesus is in me,
I am good news.

Today,
I will sow the extravagance of the gospel
everywhere I go and into everyone I meet.

Today,
I will love others as Jesus has loved me.

Today,
I will remember that the tiniest seeds become the
tallest trees; that the seeds of today become the shade
of tomorrow; that the faith of right now becomes
the future of the everlasting kingdom.

Today,
I sow for a great awakening.